EDGAR CAYCE ON

Overcoming Fear
and Anxiety

EDGAR CAYCE ON

Overcoming Fear and Anxiety

An Updated Edition of Hugh Lynn Cayce's *Faces of Fear*

HUGH LYNN CAYCE
WITH KEVIN J. TODESCHI

ARE
PRESS

ASSOCIATION FOR RESEARCH AND ENLIGHTENMENT

A.R.E. Press • Virginia Beach • Virginia

A.R.E. Press
215 67th Street
Virginia Beach, VA 23451-2061

Library of Congress Cataloguing-in-Publication Data
Cayce, Hugh Lynn.
  Edgar Cayce on overcoming fear and anxiety : an updated edition of
Hugh Lynn Cayce's Faces of fear / by Hugh Lynn Cayce with Kevin J.
Todeschi.
    p. cm.
  Includes bibliographical references (p.   ).
  ISBN 0-87604-494-1 (trade pbk.)
  1. Parapsychology and medicine. 2. Fear—Alternative treatment. 3.
Anxiety—Alternative treatment. 4. Cayce, Edgar, 1877-1945. 5. Fear. 6.
Anxiety. I. Todeschi, Kevin J. II. Cayce, Hugh Lynn. Faces of fear. III.
Title.
  BF1045.M44C39 2004
  131—dc22

                              2004020201

Cover design by Richard Boyle

Contents

The Lord is my light and my salvation; whom shall I fear?
The Lord is the strength of my life; of whom shall I be afraid?

Psalm 27:1

Foreword

THERE WAS a time when I was so terrified of speaking in front of individuals that I rarely—if ever—forced myself to even ask a question while in a group of three or more people. Except on a few occasions when I felt extremely comfortable around friends or family, I never spoke in a group and I never raised my hand in a class. When I was called on or I was forced to speak, the fear became so intense that I felt my throat constrict and grip with fear. While this occurred, breathing was next to impossible and my face would become tight and hot. Any words that did manage to escape my mouth were forced out between uneven breaths. If individuals turned to look at me as I struggled to speak, it felt as if I was strangling, choking on the words that became stuck in my throat and I would turn red-faced with embarrassment. Over the years, I became angry with myself for being so afraid and I became even more afraid of situations in which I might be called on to speak in front of people.

Today, it is almost hard to imagine being crippled by such intense fear. As a spokesperson for the work of Edgar Cayce, I have lectured in front of literally tens of thousands of individuals on five continents regarding dozens of topics. I have given dream interpretation classes in Ecuador, spoken about ancient Egypt in Japan, held intuition workshops in France, escorted numerous tour groups along the Nile, led hypnotic reveries in Canada and given hundreds of lectures throughout the United States—from California in the West and Washington D.C. in the East, and from Texas in the South and Montana in the North. The fearful student who would not even raise a hand in class could never have conceived of such a possibility.

I still remember what year I began to overcome the fear, and I clearly remember the occasion that caused me to think beyond any doubt, "I have got to do something about this." It was 1982 and I was an attendee at a retreat program in the mountains of Colorado. The speaker was Dr. Gladys McGarey, M.D., author of *Born to Live* and one of the foremost authorities of the Cayce principles of health, healing, medicine, and child rearing. Dr. Gladys, as she is affectionately known, was speaking about her many experiences during thirty-plus years as an obstetrician. I remember it was a wonderful program with about eighty of us in attendance.

As she spoke, there was a question I wanted answered that I hoped she would simply discuss. Unfortunately, she did not. As the lecture came to an end and Dr. Gladys opened the conference up for questions, I hoped that someone else would ask the question that I wanted to know. One question followed after another, each being answered in turn, but no one voiced the query that I had hoped to hear. My question was as follows: I had heard that the Edgar Cayce readings suggested whenever a child was born into the earth, the angels sang—joyously proclaiming the opportunity for spirit to enter into the earth. I wanted to know if during her many years as an obstetrician, Dr. Gladys had ever heard the music of angelic voices. That was my question, however it was a question that no one else asked.

As it became clear to me that the conference session was coming to a close, my desire to know the answer to this question became stronger than the fear of raising my hand. Feeling I had absolutely no other choice than to ask the question myself, I repeated the question in my head four or five times to reassure myself. When I had finally worked up the nerve, I raised my hand.

Immediately, Dr. Gladys called on me. I can remember sitting there ready to ask the question that I had repeatedly verbalized in my head without any problem. Suddenly, I saw three or four other conferees turn to look at me as I began to speak. Immediately, I felt my throat constrict, my face turned red, and without breathing I somehow managed to choke out a dozen words that barely provided Dr. Gladys with just enough information to know what I was really trying to ask. Even now, I can remember feeling ashamed as Dr. Gladys responded to my question, wondering how many other people had seen my public display of fear.

Synchronistically, a few weeks after the conference I had the opportunity to obtain a psychic reading from an intuitive named William Schaeffer, who was living in Denver at the time. Without thinking about my fears or worries, I went to William for a past-life reading. William and I had never met before; he knew nothing about my personal life, my hopes, my dreams, or my fears. The experience proved to be a turning point for me.

During the session, William said that one of the challenges I had to overcome in the present was a deep-seated "intolerance of intolerance." He went on to say that oftentimes in my soul's history I had gotten "up on a soapbox" to tell people about how mistaken they were in their shortsighted beliefs, their biases, and their prejudices. According to William, rather than enabling individuals to broaden their perspectives, more often than not my approach had simply gotten me "arrested, shunned, or even hanged." He added: "You know every time you get up to speak to people, your subconscious mind thinks, 'Oh no, here he goes again . . . shut him up.'" To emphasize his point, William made a hangman's noose with his fingertips and constricted the circle with his hands. At that moment, I believed I had found the cause of my fear.

To be sure, the fear did not immediately come to an end. Instead, what happened was that each time I found myself in a situation were I needed to speak before a group, I would reassure myself with positive affirmations, such as: "I have nothing to fear, I am just asking a question"; "these people want to hear what you have to say"; "there is no reason to worry, I am in a safe place," and so forth. At first, the fear was no longer crippling. Eventually, it became manageable. In time, I worked through it. William's brief statement became the catalyst that enabled me to overcome the fear that had impacted my life for as long as I could remember. Speaking in public was not my only fear, but it was certainly one of the most overwhelming.

Edgar Cayce (1877–1945), who has been called one of greatest psychics of all time, suggested that fear is one of the biggest stumblingblocks individuals face throughout their lives. Fear can be crippling; it can cause individuals to refrain from doing what they know to do and from becoming what they were meant to be. Fear comes in a variety of intensities and it seems to have a number of causes. Every individual has had to face fear at one time or another. It is the cause of fear and how we respond to that fear that sets us apart as individuals.

Throughout his life, Edgar Cayce helped countless individuals overcome every imaginable fear: fear of water, fear of ghosts, fear of the unknown, fear of failure, fear of childbirth, fear of closed-in places, fear of sex, fear of relationships, fear of weapons—every imaginable personal fear. Somehow, in his trance state, Cayce was able to get to the root cause of an individual's fear and consistently provide each person with a practical approach for overcoming fear, anxiety, and worry. In a very real sense, this information has touched the lives of thousands— not only those individuals who had readings from Edgar Cayce but also those who came after Cayce was gone and were simply able to explore the material for themselves.

Because fear is universal, Edgar Cayce's eldest son, Hugh Lynn Cayce (1907–1982), decided to publish a book in 1980 entitled *Faces of Fear* that detailed his many years of working with his father's information, assisting individuals in overcoming their personal anxieties and fears. The book contained many of Hugh Lynn's experiences overcoming his own fears. I first read *Faces of Fear* in 1982, shortly after my encounter with William Schaeffer. Hugh Lynn's volume proved to be extremely helpful in my own life. So helpful, in fact, that I never forgot it—I remembered much of the information even years after the volume had gone out of print.

Based upon on his years of experience, Hugh Lynn believed that all fears could essentially be traced to five different sources. Although some fears might have more than one cause, Hugh Lynn believed that the five major sources of fear were as follows:

- Fears due to a physical situation or problem
- Repressed fears from childhood
- Fears of religion or God
- Fears of death or the unknown
- Fears due to a past-life experience

Hugh Lynn's *Faces of Fear* would become for him one culmination of his decades of working with his father's psychic information. He delighted in talking about the book, in leading lectures and workshops about the information, and in providing individuals with tools they could utilize to overcome their own fears and anxieties. Unfortunately, the volume would be Hugh Lynn's last publication; he died from complication of cancer at the age of seventy-five on July 4, 1982.

Hugh Lynn's book was not my first experience with him. In fact, years before even graduating from college I had received a letter from him. At the time, I had written him, describing my deep interest in the Edgar Cayce information. I had long heard his name, first as his father's son, then as the general editor of a series of Warner paperbacks (the "Edgar Cayce on . . ." series) written in the late 1960s, and finally as head of the Association for Research and Enlightenment, Inc.—A.R.E., the organization founded by Edgar Cayce in 1931 to preserve, research, and disseminate his psychic information.

Imagine my surprise when, as a young man, I received a personal letter with the return address of Hugh Lynn Cayce, "A.R.E. Chairman of the Board." Hugh Lynn encouraged me to look him up when I came to Virginia Beach—something I eventually did. Years later, I discovered that Hugh Lynn's reaching out to me was not an isolated event. He often went out of his way to encourage young people to become more involved with his father's work and information.

It is important to point out that any book or publication written about Edgar Cayce and the Cayce information before the widespread use of computers was not an easy undertaking. When Hugh Lynn was alive, researching the Cayce readings could be a painstaking experience, sifting through literally hundreds or even thousands of pages looking for a certain quote or a particular case history. It was a process that could take days, weeks, or even months. The advent of the Cayce readings on CD-ROM in the 1990s made a manual search of the Cayce files a thing of the past. Individual words and phrases contained within the more than 14,000 readings could be discovered in an instant. In a very real sense, Hugh Lynn Cayce and those who knew Edgar Cayce personally did not have access to the Cayce information in ways that we do today.

As the years passed and I began to see how many others were affected by a variety of fears, I remembered how very helpful Hugh Lynn's book had been in my own life. On several occasions I mentioned that it was too bad the book had gone out of print. I hoped that, in time, something could be done to make Hugh Lynn's volume and the Cayce information on fear more readily available to others. Finally, because of my own background in writing and the Cayce information, I was asked to help make the material available once again.

This publication gives access to Hugh Lynn's information to new generations. With the exception of more references from the Cayce readings, some additional material drawn from Hugh Lynn's public talks, the discarding of dated references, and a brief foreword, this volume is very much Hugh Lynn Cayce's original *Faces of Fear*. Although the book has been reissued and updated, it remains the culmination of Hugh Lynn's life and work. The material is still timely, helpful, insightful, and a source of inspiration for overcoming life's fears and anxieties from the perspective of the Edgar Cayce information.

I hope you will find, as I have, that fear is not a state of mind with which an individual is forever burdened but can instead be a learning experience and a process that most individuals—given the proper tools and insight—can work through.

By the way, in 1982 when I asked Dr. Gladys about whether or not she had ever heard the angel's sing during a child's birth, she paused, seemed to ponder the question for a moment, looked around the room and finally replied: "Yes . . . many times."

Perhaps there is much more to us than we have ever dared to imagine.

Kevin J. Todeschi

1

The Nature of Fear

Keep thine face toward the light, and the shadows will not bring fright—for fear is the beginning of all undoing.   2056-2

THE PIECES of paper on the table in front of me blurred through my tears. Thoughts flashed through my consciousness like streaks of lightning. Why should I cry? It was World War II and millions of men were separated from their loved ones. Thousands were dying here in France and to the north and east. The faces of the bloated bodies we had seen along the roads, after the breakthrough at Saint-Lô, came back to me. Yes, my father, Edgar Cayce, was dead and my mother was dying. A V-Mail from my brother on an island in the Caribbean had been the first word of my father's death (the Battle of the Bulge was on), with news that Dad had been buried in Hopkinsville, Kentucky. Now a Red Cross message stated that my wife, the mother of our son—less than two years old—was in the hospital. According to the doctor, I

1

should expect and prepare for the worst.

Maybe if I could pray I could stand the depression that was sweeping over me. I got up and went out into the hall of the old, French chateau where our company of 125 men was quartered. A short distance away, heavy canvases were stretched across the hall. Beyond was open space, where part of the building had been bombed away. I pushed the canvas aside and slipped through. Here I could be alone. Already it was getting dark and it was raining, a cold drizzle. I stopped well back from the edge of the crumbling floor and stood there trying to pray.

Where was God? How could a loving Father let this happen? The depression deepened. If there was ever a God, maybe He had gone away to another part of the universe, leaving the earth and everything, including humanity, to fend for itself. Maybe there wasn't anything out there. Was it all a coincidence, a fluke of nature, meaningless, all ending in nothingness? This madness in which we were involved made no sense. Suddenly everything that I believed in was washed out of me— God, love, Jesus, service. Empty, alone, and cut off from my family, I could find no meaning in life. I was desolate, and I was afraid.

I do not know how long I stayed in that place or in that state of mind. Finally, I forced myself to pray, "God, if You are there, hear me. Let me keep my wife; our son needs her. *I need her.* If in my weakness I cannot serve You, use our son." Over and over again, I thought and muttered these and similar words. Later, I talked with a friend about how I felt, and he prayed for me. After a sleepless night that resembled the feeling one gets from a nightmare, I forced myself to relax by suggestion and finally to begin to meditate. Even that didn't seem to help. It was one of the most difficult episodes in my life; it would be two weeks before I learned that my wife's operation had disclosed a benign tumor and not a malignancy, as had been feared.

Over the years there has been plenty of time for me to consider this experience again and again. Repeatedly, I have gone back to it in my mind. How could a person like me suddenly be afraid and doubt the existence of God? My family background had provided religious train- ing, Bible study, and church activity. The constant example of a mother and father who not only worshiped but also believed in a loving Cre- ator was always before me. For ten years our family had studied and worked in a Disciples of Christ church in Selma, Alabama. My father was the best Sunday school teacher I'd ever met. Following his example, I had become involved in a growing, young Presbyterian church when our family moved to Virginia Beach, Virginia, in 1925. We had worked in the church with a young, open-minded, dedicated minister. God had always been a very réal Presence in my life.

Moreover, my father's amazing ability as a psychic and remarkably helpful medical clairvoyant provided enough evidence for me, again and again, that God could and did work through individuals to continue to bring healing, spiritual insight, and meaning to life. For years I had been involved in Boy Scout work, not just as a community service but also as a way of helping growing boys. When I had been drafted into the army—far too old, I thought, at thirty-four—I had been actively working with a group studying prayer and meditation. I had seen average people like me change dysfunctional life patterns in helpful and beautiful ways. Some individuals had become more creative, many were able to face difficulties and obstacles with greater courage, others had ceased to be critical, and countless individuals had found that they were able to work with forgiveness. One member of my group had developed the knack for helpful and precognitive dreams; another had experiences of instantaneous healing for herself and others. Through a variety of personal experiences, I had become certain that God was at work in the world. In my own way, I had shared many insights from my father's readings, which had helped individuals refocus their lives in more creative service.

Even in the face of everything I knew and believed, and all that I had been brought up with, I become afraid, paralyzed, and filled with doubt that life had any meaning at all. I began to drink excessively. Prayer and meditation became intermittent.

When the war was over, I returned home to become manager, then president, and finally chairman of the board of the A.R.E. (Association for Research and Enlightenment, Inc.), the educational, membership organization founded in 1931 to explore, research, and disseminate information contained in the Edgar Cayce readings. Perhaps, in part, because of my experience overseas, with my return I made a special effort to examine the Cayce information on fear.

The first time I really made an effort to make this information available to a wider audience was in 1953, when A.R.E. sponsored a conference of lectures and workshops that focused on understanding and
transforming fear patterns of the body and mind into more constructive channels of activity. As I read both the Edgar Cayce material and
the literature on fear, I very soon recognized that rather than being
entirely detrimental there were many usable, helpful kinds of fear. In
fact, some had actually preserved and helped humankind throughout
history.

For example, it had certainly been helpful in the course of human
evolution for people to fear growling, hungry tigers; just as it was important for modern individuals to be cautious of crowded highways
and speeding cars. Along the same lines, the fear of punishment had
often restrained individuals from committing crimes, such as vandal-
ism, stealing, or even killing. Certainly the fear of "what people might
say" has served to mold many crude, primitive tendencies into patterns
that are more acceptable to society as a whole. However, what about
common crippling fears we all know? Where did those fears come from?
What can individuals do about fears of the unknown or the fear of
failure? Is there a cure for the fear that life has no meaning? Can repressed fears or fears that seem to be held deep within the subconscious be eradicated or transformed?

There is such a wide range of things that make people anxious or
worried that I remember once, when I was on an airplane to the West
Coast and trying to do something to pass the time, I made a list of
literally dozens of fears. In brief, my listing included the following: fear
of death, loneliness, a particular person, an animal, insect or reptile, and
monsters of the mind (from dreams or drug experiences). There is the
fear of falling, of drowning, of earth calamity, destruction or war. Individuals can be afraid of close places, of heights, of smothering, and of
the dark. Common fears often include the fear of sickness, cancer, the
unknown, damnation, facing God, and the devil. There are fears of poverty, of other groups of people (terrorists, for example), of pain, and of
weapons (such as knives or guns). People fear relationships, sexual inadequacy, ridicule, job failure, public speaking, making changes, and
flying. There is every imaginable fear that humans can become sub-

jected to—from fear of parenthood to the fear of the meaninglessness of life, to the fear of noises and the fear of getting lost.

My work with attempting to understand the nature of human fears led me to the unmistakable conclusion that each of these is only one of the faces of fear. Behind all of the "faces" there was a basic cause or underlying factor that was the real root of the fear. Actually, if a fear is to become transformed or overcome, it is to the underlying factors and causes that an individual must direct her or his attention.

When I first decided to interview one hundred young people about their most memorable fear experience, I discovered that—regardless of how the fear had manifested—their fears were remarkably similar to some of the most commonly acknowledged fears of society in general. Their experiences reflected the fear of death, failure, the meaningless-ness of life, the unknown, personal inadequacy, the fear of what people may think, etc. (Thankfully, suggestions from my father's psychic infor-mation proved to be extremely helpful for many of them.) The follow-ing examples illustrate just a few of the countless fear experiences that were related to me.

Example 1: *A twenty-five-year-old's dream that seemed to depict the fear of getting lost and being unable to discover personal, spiritual meaning:*

Dream—I seemed to be in a junkyard; it was very dim and dingy. In searching around I saw a light bulb hanging down from a cord, with a pull-chain. I pulled the chain and the light came on, though dim and of a low wattage. I had my *A Search for God* book in my hand. I rummaged and searched around for a few minutes, and then suddenly realized I had lost or dropped the book. With a sickening feeling of panic in my stomach, I wildly moved this and that, looking for the book and berating myself for my carelessness. Suddenly, the light went out.

I then seemed to be plunging or moving through the darkness—I could see nothing—it seemed just space. I began saying the affirmation, "Not my will but Thine, O Lord, be done in me and through me . . . " I awakened, praying, in a cold sweat.

Example 2: *A sixteen-year-old student described an experience that combined fear of father with a fear of failure:*

Well, the worst experience I've ever had was with my father. When I lived with him, he used to get drunk and throw me around all over the place. He could not control himself when he was drunk, and he did everything to make up for what he did when he was sober. Finally, he started insulting me so badly—he said I was ruining his life, his business, his marriage, everything. This hurt me very deeply, obviously, so I left.

Example 3: *A drug-induced experience in which fear of losing control was related by a young man who claimed that at sixteen he had taken drugs at least a hundred times. He told me that he would never use drugs again because of the fear generated in the following experience:*

Well, let's put it this way—I saw the light. I had a bad experience, too. The mellow sensation came first on this particular trip. I had a peaceful view toward everything. It opened my mind in this sense. Something in that trip made me realize that if I got over the bridge I would be okay. Several times, though, during the trip, I started to lose control. And I knew that if I did lose control, that would be it. My mind would have completely gone the wrong route. I just struggled for control and got it. I was afraid of what would happen if I lost control.

Example 4: *A conscious dream or vision experience of a twenty-eight-year-old, who encountered a symbol of death and became afraid. It seems to have been a warning dream that helped change an attitude about the individual—who had been neglecting the physical body—becoming a constructive fear experience in the process:*

Daydream—This was about three weeks ago. This was just before I got ill with pneumonia. About two days before this pneumonia attack occurred, this dark figure appeared. It was more of a dream/ vision, but a very conscious one. This figure appeared and the first thing he said was, "Are you ready to die?" and I said, "No." I had a long conversation with this spirit of death. But the amazing thing was that he was really scary because it was dark. But I knew that even though he was dark, that somehow there was goodwill in him. And then he said, "Just because I don't tell you doesn't mean that I don't know." He repeated that many times. Like he knew whatever it was I needed to know, but he wasn't telling me. This really changed me; I no longer treat the physical body so lightly.

Example 5: *A twelve-year-old girl discussed having to face a fear because of peer pressure. Obviously her fear of what her friends might think became stronger than her fear of the situation. She was standing on the end of a diving board ten feet above the water in a park lake. She was being urged by her friends to jump. She was excited, hesitated, then cried out, "I'm afraid." She finally leaped off the board and came up sputtering.*

Example 6: *A twenty-five-year-old was asked to relate the worst experience he ever had. He immediately remembered a dream that had occurred as a child:*

When I was real little, about six or seven, I woke up in the middle of the night and my parents came in, and I was standing in the bed screaming—I was having some kind of really bad nightmare, like almost hysterical. I don't remember the dream or what it was all about, but I do remember the experience.

Additional common fear examples included: the fear of speaking in public, perhaps stemming from the fear of embarrassment or the fear of appearing ridiculous. Some discussed the fear of being alone. Many individuals described the fear of sexual inadequacy. For others the devil was very real, a force of evil to be feared. Poverty or the loss of money seemed to be a haunting fear for a few. Other universal fears included the fear of pain, death, and the unknown.

During my exploration into the nature of fear, I took the opportunity to interview younger children at our association's summer camp programs. Once these youngsters understood that I was willing to listen to them, they talked freely about a variety of childhood fears. Some were afraid of members of their families; others feared snakes and spiders. One boy thought he had seen people who were dead and was afraid of them. Underneath the surface, their fears proved to be more complex, such as fears of dying, fears of war, and fears of not being accepted by their peers.

As a means of trying to understand the basis of childhood fears, which many individuals carry with them throughout life, a questionnaire was developed and distributed to approximately fifty young adults. Certainly, the questionnaire has no statistical significance. Instead, it was simply an attempt to see if any fears would be repeatedly mentioned as being of the greatest concern to these individuals. The majority of participants were simply young people who were visiting the A.R.E. in Virginia Beach. From a list of sixty-two fears, the five that were checked most frequently were as follows:

- Fear of failure
- Fear of meaninglessness
- Fear of rejection
- Fear of war
- Fear of loneliness

Later surveys were developed for literally hundreds of individuals from adult audiences. In time, those surveys would result in a summation of the five fears that seemed most evident in adults: (1) fears due to a physical situation or problem; (2) repressed fears from childhood; (3) fears of religion or God; (4) fears of death or the unknown; and, (5) fears due to a past-life experience. Eventually, a questionnaire was also created as a means of assisting individuals in exploring the possible basis of their own fears. (See Appendix A: "Fear Questionnaire: Getting in Touch with Possible Causes for Personal Fears.")

In the process of working with literally thousands of individuals, it has become evident that the things we fear are not necessarily in themselves causes. Rather, they are often undefined anxieties, unrelated to the present. In fact, we can unconsciously create fears in our minds to avoid dealing adequately with the present as well as to avoid whatever the real root issue may be. Edgar Cayce told a sixty-five-year-old woman in 1941 that, "Fear is that element in the character and in the experience of individuals which brings about more of trouble than any other influence in the experience of an entity." (2560-1) In order to transform our fears, we must come to grips with what is causing them in the first place.

Psychologists, physicians, students, and individuals from every imaginable background and life experience have studied this information. In that process, many have found that the Edgar Cayce material on fear parallels and supports concepts of some of the best literature available in the field. The readings clearly articulate the belief that our separation from God can produce guilt, loneliness, and a feeling of meaninglessness in life. They also contain examples in which guilt and conflict arise from childhood suppressions that become the source of many fears.

However, the Cayce materials also explore some fears that seem to have a physical basis, as well as fears that appear to be connected to distorted perceptions about the physical body. For example, a forty-seven-year-old M.D. with several medical problems was told that an incoordination between his cerebrospinal and sympathetic nervous systems was causing dizziness, nausea, and a fear of high places. Among other things, the readings recommended osteopathic adjustments and internal medications (1052-1).

In addition, the readings examine unique information regarding how deeper memories of past lives can often be at the root of present-day fear patterns. As one example, a forty-year-old woman was told that her extreme fear of lightning was traced to a wartime experience in which her husband had been defeated by an opposing army. Apparently the sounds of thunder subconsciously reminded her of the sounds of war, and the nervous reaction she had faced in the past returned to her in the present. The readings advised her to use her will power and her faith to overcome the problem. In this manner, it would become less and less of an issue to her mental and physical health (1602-1).

Finally, the Cayce information offers some exciting new ideas on overcoming the fear of death, dying, and the unknown. In the case of a twenty-three-year-old woman, who apparently had a fear of death,

Cayce told her that some of her dreams were directly connected to her fear. In the dreams, the woman repeatedly came in contact and communicated with individuals who were deceased. The readings told her that the dreams where to assure her of two things: that death was not the end; and, that communication between herself and her deceased loved ones was possible. The dreams had occurred in order to assist her in overcoming her fears (136–73).

For literally decades, I have made a special effort to share concepts from my father's readings on fear. During that time I believe I have learned a little not only about fear but also, I hope, about helping people use their energy in more productive ways. Rather than being a crippling influence in life, the energy of fear can be channeled into healing directions, freeing individuals to become more loving and more aware of their relationship to themselves, one another, and their God. With this information, many people seemed to have been helped by being able to better understand the cause of their fear and how it operates in their lives, and by using techniques from the readings to transform fear energy into something much more creative and helpful.

The purpose of this book is to share this material, making these practical, helpful insights available to others.

2

Are Our Bodies Afraid?

Where it has taken years to produce a fear, a doubt, an activity that begins to find manifestation in the twitching of a muscle, in the expansion of a vein, in the frustrations in the body forces—be patient, be quiet within; and we will find those administrations that have been made—and that may be made—will aid thee in growing in the right directions.   3051-3

SUDDENLY, AN uncontrollable fear surged through my whole body. A knot formed in my muscles and nerves of my solar plexus. My throat grew dry. I began to choke. The muscles in my thighs and the calves of my legs grew tense and then began to quiver violently. Terror-stricken, I crouched against the rough, huge blocks of limestone halfway up the northeast corner of the Great Pyramid of Gizeh.

My guide, Ahmed, stopped and looked back at me. He pointed to the path on which he had moved over the blocks of stone and reached down to steady me. Paralyzed, I clung to rough places on the stones. "I'll rest," I told him. My friends from our tour group climbed on above me. They called out that it was easier going near the top.

After a few minutes of labored breathing, I looked up and knew I could not go on. I signaled Ahmed and began to slide and crawl back down the side of the pyramid. By the time I reached the bottom, steadied from time to time by Ahmed, I had broken into a cold sweat. Meanwhile, my friends had reached the top.

I sat down and tried to think. My body reactions amazed me. Never before, so far as I could remember, had I been afraid of heights. I felt frustrated, ashamed, and angry with myself. Slowly, as my body stopped sweating and my limbs stopped quivering, I forced myself to think of starting again up the side of the pyramid. No one else in our group seemed to have any trouble. The guides were as much at home on the rocks as on the level ground. I closed my eyes and began to pray silently for understanding. Then, of itself, my mind shifted to a familiar psalm: "Who shall ascend into the hill of the Lord . . . he that hath clean hands and a pure heart" (Psalm 24:3).

Without thinking of the incongruity of the words and my plight, I released my fear. My body relaxed, and my mind became calm. I held on to the peace, letting my mind come back again and again to the words of the psalm, then letting myself experience the quietness that came with them. For ten minutes, I sat there while Ahmed waited patiently. Then I stood up, gave him some more money and, with his help over the high places, climbed to the top of the Great Pyramid to join my friends.

Later, as I reflected on what had happened, I could not consciously find an answer to the cause of the experience. It was almost as if my body had separated from my mind. My body was afraid; the paralysis, choking, and sweating had all occurred spontaneously. Does the body itself have memory in its very cells? Had I brought this fear over from some forgotten childhood incident? And what had enabled me to transform the energy, which had stopped every movement of my limbs, so that I could climb to the very top of the pyramid?

Within the Edgar Cayce material, we can find examples of fear patterns that seem to arise from cellular memory, patterns biologically associated with anxiety and fear. Apparently, various body tissues are capable of acquiring memories that can be automatically stimulated to respond to a fixed pattern. Later, we will explore how the endocrine glands, which affect practically all bodily functions, are especially involved in our "memory" system. And some cases from the Edgar Cayce files suggest that spinal injuries or glandular imbalances can actually trigger anxiety and fear.

In 1921, in giving a reading to a woman that had problems with her spine and circulation due to the aftereffects of an injury, Cayce said that her fear "spells" were the result of an accident that had occurred nearly a decade earlier. Not only was there pressure along her spine and an incoordination of her circulation but her heart and blood supply often tried to overcompensate to throw off the excess pressure that had resulted after the accident. Cayce described the problem, in part, as follows: " . . . it brings a rush of blood to the head filling the upper cavities of the lungs, so that the breath is quick, fast and hard, and the head becomes filled so that the forces of the mind are impaired. That is, it is fear, more than an actual condition." (4667-1)

In addition to having a physical impact upon her body, the condition was also responsible for hallucinations that the woman was having. Various manipulative therapies were suggested designed to correct the pressure along her spine, relieve the circulatory problems and bring her relief from the condition. In this instance, the woman's anxiety and fear were connected to a spinal injury. Numerous such examples are found in the Edgar Cayce readings.

In a case from 1930, a wife obtained a reading for her husband who suffered from a variety of problems, many of which the readings traced to various physical difficulties. The husband complained about personal fears, low self-esteem, depression, intolerance of others, anxiety about the future, sleeplessness, impatience, and suicidal tendencies. The reading began by suggesting many of his mental problems had a physical basis: "In the physical there are disturbances that cause conditions that, in their reaction, produce definite reactions in the mental." (5437-1) Beginning with improper eliminations throughout the blood supply, affecting both assimilation and digestion, Cayce stated that this problem combined with the individual's frequent self–condemnation had contributed to problems with irregular heartbeat, shortness of breath and physical strain throughout the body systems and even "distortions" of the mind. Taken together, these imbalances were contributing to his various fears.

In order to address the individual's condition, the readings suggested that both physical therapies and a change in mental outlook would be necessary. To this end, recommendations included massage, internal medications, therapies designed to increase the flow of oxygen through–out his body and chiropractic adjustments to the "8th and 9th dorsal, the 3rd and 4th dorsal, [and] the 3rd and 5th cervical." Cayce assured the individual and his wife that if these recommendations were followed, he would begin to notice a change in his outlook, health, and wellbeing in a very short period of time.

After receiving these suggestions, the question was asked, "Why has [5437] a fear of the future? Why does he not want to live?" The reading responded:

> The natural tendency of the gnawing from within, and the natural pressure created in the upper portion of system from same, distorts the *view* of the body, as well as those of depressions from the associations *about* same, but with a *physical* outlook changed, the whole outlook of body—mentally *and* physically—will also be changed. Will these but be applied, we will see great *changes* in this body, mentally and physically, in three weeks. Not perfectly well, no—for then, as has been given, there should be a change in the *physical* outlook, or a change in the physical surroundings for a time.   5437-1

Another example of physical problems being cited as the cause of an individual's fears occurred in the case of a sixty–one–year–old woman who was suffering from depression, anxiety, and a fear of noises. In describing her condition, Cayce stated, " . . . most of the nerve system and systems are involved, as well as the assimilating and eliminating system, as related to the blood supply and of the functioning organs, as has to do with this portion of the physical body." (5629-1) In part, the readings suggested that the woman was suffering from nerve exhaustion. When she asked, "Why have I such fear of noises?" The response was that it was caused by "the improper coordination between the cerebrospinal and sympathetic system."

In this instance, her reading advised against internal medications, suggesting that her body would react adversely to them. Instead, the recommendations included lots of rest, external adjustments, a change of diet that was more alkaline in nature, and the use of electrical appliances designed to stimulate and normalize her body's circulation.

Another example of fears being connected to physical problems occurred in 1943. After reading Edgar Cayce's biography, *There is a River*, a thirty-eight-year-old woman wrote asking for Cayce's help and advice. Her letter said, in part:

> For over three years I have been more or less isolated from my former participation in an active enjoyment of social contacts. I have suffered from the pains which seem to come from a spinal curvature, plus what has variously been termed a "nervous break-down," menopause, malnutrition, and even some type of infantile [paralysis]. After many months in bed I attempted to fight my way back to normalcy, but had developed a tendency to have a "complex" about being in the company of my friends, dreading callers and finding it almost an impossibility to walk out of sight of my home, as I have a horrible physical experience each time I have attempted these things. I have had many doctors, including orthopedic men, psychiatrists and Christian Science practitioners. I am not bed-ridden, but am active with many hobbies at home such as gardening, music, painting, photography and development and tinting work, and work for the Red Cross which I can do at home.
>
> My husband [...] is on active sea duty, and it would be a great relief to him to know that I am once more able to be without fear, and restored to my natural state of self reliance, as I have to call upon others to stay with me when he is away.
>
> 3061-1 Report File

The woman's questions included the following: "What causes the nervous sense of fright and how can it be overcome?" "Why am I so frightened and apprehensive all the time, so that I fear company and yet fear to be alone?" "What causes the tension in neck and dizziness?" "What causes sharp pain under the rib area?" and, "Can the spine be helped? How?"

In beginning the reading, Cayce said that her fear and anxiety was a combination of conditions resulting from disturbances along the lower areas of her cerebrospinal system. These disturbances were also causing a "sympathetic" response in her nerve forces, her torso and even her mobility. In addition to the above, the problem was being accentuated because of "warring forces" in her own mind in which she was torn between falling victim to her fears and overcoming the disability.

In order to address the physical problems and help her relax, the readings recommended osteopathic adjustments, gentle exercise, foods rich with vitamins A and D, hydrotherapy, and external packs over the spinal cord. Cayce said these packs would act, "as an alkalizing antiseptic, as well as being absorbed in the muscular tendons and lymph circulation so as to alkalize and eliminate." To help her mental state of mind, the readings also suggested reading uplifting verse from scripture, specifically, "the 30th of Deuteronomy, and the 14th, 15th, 16th and 17th of John." By following these suggestions, Cayce assured her that she would find relief from her anxieties and physical problems.

In 1933, a thirty-three-year-old hotel manager, who had received previous readings from Edgar Cayce, wrote to describe a series of nervous attacks that had been plaguing him. He described his condition, as follows:

I have been sort of sick mentally. Not as badly, I'm glad to say, as I used to be, but just a little down in the mouth and despondent. I have had only one "attack" lately, and that was just the other evening. I was home alone reading a paper when I had a peculiar feeling around the eyes, as though my eyes wanted to close and couldn't. Then, a sort of numbness in the head, and immediately following a short dizzy sensation, followed by a wild palpitation of my heart. Being alone, I was more or less frantic. But, I went

to the medicine cabinet, took a sedative pill, and lay down on the bed. I quieted down in a few moments, and felt a little better. About five minutes later, that same dizzy feeling, and the palpitation. I called the doctor from downstairs, and he came up in a few minutes, and listened to my heart. Told me there was nothing wrong organically, but that I was quite nervous. He attributed it all to nerves. I pray to the Lord that I can overcome these terrible ordeals. I have had about four of these spells, almost exactly alike each time, in the last eight or nine months.

                                                    279-18 Report File

Cayce provided a reading and suggested that the condition could be called "nerve reaction, or nervousness, neurasthenia" and would be greatly improved by a coordination between the sympathetic and cerebrospinal systems of the body. To this end, he recommended manipulative therapies and relaxation techniques including baths, massage, and salt rubs. The individual was also encouraged to use his imaginative forces and focus on positive imagery that would help him overcome his fears. By so doing, he could make great strides in learning to "master self"—learning to refrain from allowing himself to give into the fear impulse. He was also encouraged to find more balance in his life. In addition, Cayce encouraged him to follow a diet that had been previously recommended, consisting, in part, of the following:

Mornings—citrus fruits, with wafers or toast, and occasionally a coddled egg; but do not mix cereals with citrus fruits, though at times this may be changed to stewed fruits, baked apple, prunes and figs, and such. These would be well for the morning . . .

Noon, or lunch—this should be rather light, preferably a mixed green vegetable diet, altered at times with broths or soups—as vegetable soups . . .

Evenings—would be of the cooked vegetables, and with fish, chicken, mutton and beef, provided it is not in grease. Do not take too much of any fried prepared foods, that has the fried or the fats in same. Those that are boiled, stewed or broiled, may be taken very well.   279-1

When the individual asked whether or not he had cause to fear "a severe mental breakdown," Cayce replied:

> No cause whatever, if the body will more and more surround self with those suggestive influences that it innately knows and feels, that may be manifested between a Creative influence into the material and mental life of a body; for it may make of itself that it will, in the mental or material world.   279-18

A fifty-four-year-old woman was told that her physical problems and mental worries had resulted because of "a subluxation in the cerebrospinal system, that first affected the activity of the liver as related to both heart and the kidneys." From Cayce's perspective, this problem had resulted in the fact that "most every organ is disturbed in its reaction in some way or manner." (1645-1) In addition to her physical systems being affected, the problem had created fears, anxieties, and worries that "this or that may occur."

The readings outlined a regimen of treatment that included osteopathic adjustments in the upper dorsal and the ninth dorsal and the fourth lumbar. Cayce stated that these adjustments would "gradually remove the strain upon the system." In addition, the woman was informed that the subluxations had resulted in a large accumulation of waste materials in her ascending colon and prescribed a series of colonic irrigations and enemas to correct the problem. In terms of diet, the woman was encouraged to drink large quantities of juices (fruit, vegetable, and beef) until her system had corrected the elimination problem.

In addition to the above, she was encouraged to have constructive thoughts:

> *Don't feel sorry for self!* Know that the conditions which exist are a part of thy experience! Use them as stepping-stones, not as stumbling-stones!
>
> Let the body, then, be filled with the desire to be good; not merely good but good *for* something—for others! Quit thinking of self! Think of doing something constructive for someone else!
>   1645-1

By following these suggestions, Cayce assured her, "If these are done persistently, consistently, we will find bettered conditions for this body."

In 1938, a sixty–four–year–old woman had sent Mr. Cayce questions asking about her own physical problems and feelings of fear and anxiety:

> My whole body is full of pain, especially in the joints, is sensitive to touch and I have great difficulty in walking, this condition is growing worse, what is the cause and what shall I do for it?
>
> I have a continuous headache and pain at the back of the neck what do you advise to cure it?
>
> I suffer from depression and fear, fear of my condition and a fear of life and people.
>
> I do not sleep without a sedative, what shall I do to regain normal sleep.
>
> I am constipated what is the remedy?
>
> I have a constant nagging pain in the lower abdomen, is hard to locate is it from a nervous condition? What shall I do for it?
>
> Any help and light on my condition will be most gratefully received.   1756-1 Report File

Her reading suggested corrective measures for each problem. For her headache and pain, the reading's recommendations include osteopathic adjustments, massage, and Epsom salt baths. The depression and fear were attributed to pressures along the sympathetic nervous system, and would be assisted by the adjustments and improvements to her circulation. Problems with sleep would cease after having a series of adjustments and by relaxing with the Epsom salts baths. The constipation could be remedied with the use of enemas. A diet that refrained from starches, breads, and potatoes and was instead rich with nuts, fruits, and vegetables was also recommended. Finally, the "nagging pain" in her lower abdomen was attributed to an "incoordination between the upper and lower hepatic circulation"; it would also be corrected by following the same suggestions.

Another example of fear being connected to a physical condition came in the form of a fifty–four–year–old woman who complained of bad headaches and her fears of being left alone and of the dark. Cayce informed her that the problems had come about as the aftereffects of an accident that had caused subluxations in the cervical and coccyx areas of her spine. Cayce described the cause of her fear, as follows: "Thus through the areas these press upon the nerves and produce tiredness; while those in the cervical area are of such a nature to produce fear— especially of being alone, or of the dark, or of heights, or of those things that become as fearful experiences for individuals." (2825-1) As was often the case, recommendations included osteopathy, the use of an electrical appliance to stimulate circulation, and a heating pad or hot packs applied to the spine.

These cases suffice to make the point that Edgar Cayce sometimes traced troublesome fear sensations to distorted perceptions arising from physical malfunctions in the nerve systems. Again and again, when corrections within the physical body were made, the fear sensations were eliminated.

To be sure, the Cayce information frequently discussed the important role mental thoughts and attitudes played in contributing to fears as well as overcoming them. For example, in 1930 a widow with three young children was told that that her mind was contributing to both her physical problems and her worries: "Worry and fear being, then, the greatest foes to *normal* healthy physical body, turning the assimilated forces in the system into poisons that must be eliminated, rather than into life giving vital forces for a physical body." (5497-1) In addition to physical therapies, the readings recommended spending time in open spaces, staying away from crowds and hectic situations, eating a balanced diet, and spending time in spiritual pursuits or activities that would cultivate her faith in God.

Along the same lines, in 1944 a fifty-one-year-old woman was warned just how detrimental a negative attitude could be upon her body: "If there are the worries and aggravations, these worries and aggravations will reflect in the functioning of the organs of the central nerve and blood supply as well as in the sympathetic." (338-9) Advice included working with her mental attitude and the application of her spiritual beliefs and ideals.

Another example is the case of a twenty-four-year-old woman, who had often taken sedatives to help relax her anxieties and worries. Cayce informed her that her ongoing difficulties—including insomnia and nervousness—were no longer as much a physical condition as they were a result of her mental attitude. When she asked, "What can I do to be less nervous?" Cayce replied: "More and more employ self in doing something that will bring to others that the body feels will be a pleasure to them. Do not pity self. Do not be angry at self." (911-4) She was also advised not to worry that her condition was taking longer to heal than she desired, and to begin trying to be less reliant on sedatives, which were creating additional toxins that had to be eliminated from her already overly taxed physical systems.

The woman inquired as to which sedatives she could use; to which the reading responded that she should refrain from using them, whenever possible. Apparently, she had become so reliant on the sedatives that she was having to take ever greater quantities to have the same effect. Cayce told her: " . . . do not build more and more, and more and more; rather fight to make it less and less, and less." In response, she asked, "When shall I eliminate sedatives and hypnotics entirely?" The reply came, "When the body has builded within self that determination 'I will *not!*' and then *does not!*" To this end, Cayce recommended that she begin using the following affirmation:

> *There is being created within my system, through the normal impulses from the organs of my body, a balance that is normal! Normal to others as well as myself!*
>
> *That the system has become so that it relies upon other influences I know, but I will be the boss!"*

A different kind of cause for distorted perceptions, yet also connected to the physical, was described in numerous Edgar Cayce readings related to glandular disturbances in the endocrine system. When the treatments suggested were followed, the fear sensations stopped.

One example occurred in 1941 in the case of a thirty-six-year-old woman. According to Cayce, her problem of nervousness, including the fear of childbirth, had been triggered by glandular disturbances resulting from improper care at birth. Cayce described the source of the problem, as follows:

> The sources or causes of the glandular reaction in the lacteals are from a pressure produced there during those periods when there was the care for the umbilical cord or center, by too great a pressure, and a cold or congestion that once caused some inflammation, during those first ten to fifteen days of the body-physical development.   2441-1

Recommended treatments included exercises that would stretch her abdominal muscles, massages in the area extending from her lower ribs to her lower torso, and dietary recommendations that included foods with A, D, G, and B–1 vitamins. She was also encouraged to cultivate an attitude that would increase her faith that the Creative Forces could work to help heal the condition. By doing these things, Cayce assured her that she would heal the glandular imbalance, overcome her fears, and fulfill that purpose for which she had entered into the earth.

Apparently delighted with the information, shortly after receiving the reading the woman wrote Edgar Cayce a letter:

> Have you ever seen a bird that has been caged let go free! That is truly the experience that I had Wednesday the 5th when I received the physical reading which you gave me. Truly a miracle! Words are so inadequate to express everything—God Bless You is about the best I can do—Thank You seems so weak! The full significance is just beginning to sink into consciousness.

On another occasion, in 1935, a twenty–year–old male had written to explain his own desperate situation:

> This is a *plea* for help. I am about desperate and need your help more than anyone's on earth.
>
> I have a mental disorder and have been under the treatment of a psychologist at the University of [...] where I am going to school. So far I have gotten nowhere under his treatment and really am just about at the depths of discouragement.
>
> I hope that you will favor me by giving me a mental and physical reading as soon as you can. I honestly feel down in my

heart that if you can't help me, no person on earth can.

I am at home now for the holidays and will be here until the fourth or fifth of January.

Neither father or mother know of my condition and I really prefer that they not know of it.

I am sending this "special" [delivery] and am praying that you will realize how serious and important this is to me and that you will be able to give me a reading at your earliest time.

Please let me hear from you immediately because I *am* anxious and *need* your help . . .   1089-1 Report File

During the course of the reading, Cayce discussed a variety of problems that were creating fear and anxiety within the individual: dizziness, sounds of voices, memory lapses, hallucinations, and sexual dysfunction. Perhaps, surprisingly, the reading suggested that the condition was due, in part, to the individual's psychic abilities attempting to manifest. It was essentially described as the phenomenon of spiritual expressions being channeled through the physical functioning of the body. On frequent occasions, the readings attributed this type of experience to glandular functioning, since the endocrine glands were seen as points of contact between the body and the soul.

As a case in point, Cayce once stated, "There has always been a portion of the anatomical forces of the body, through which [psychic] expressions come to individual activity." (262–20) These anatomical forces are the endocrine glands. With this in mind, it is a reasonable hypothesis to suggest that if gland functions become disturbed some psychic experiences may develop. Telepathic or clairvoyant perceptions involving fear thought patterns or the activities of other people might provoke fear sensations in a sensitive person.

In this instance, the readings recommended frequent prayer and meditation to bring about balance and assured the young man that by relying upon things of the spirit, he would "snap out" of his fear and depression. The readings went on to suggest that the young man was not crazy but that he had the potential to be used as a channel of psychic and spiritual information for others.

In another case, a thirty–year–old female artist obtained a reading because of panic attacks, a fear of going out by herself and anxiety about traveling on trains—a mode of transportation that was essential at the time for her carrying about her work. According to her reading's request:

> I don't know quite how to explain my trouble ... It started almost a year ago; it seems to be nerves, but I have a terrible fear of trains and going out by myself; as my job necessitates train travel to [...] I live each day in constant fear that I shall have to go. When one of these attacks comes on I feel as though I were going to leave my body and the fear is terrible. They come on even when I am going to a familiar place, now, whereas before they only seemed to occur when I went to a new place ... It is ruining health and my opportunities and I do not seem to be able to fight it. I have tried everything I know. I have forced myself to do things but it doesn't help. Now this feeling comes more frequently and without much apparent cause. I'm afraid I am not being very clear about this thing, but I do ask you please to find out what I can do to cure myself. I cannot stand this panic much longer and feel that I am in for some kind of breakdown ... all I want to know is how to stop this fear ...   **2114-1 Report File**

During the course of the reading, Cayce described symptoms such as an inability to concentrate or rest, being overly excitable, trembling, problems with irregular circulation, and the presence of fears, inhibitions, and doubts. The reading pinpointed the cause of the disturbances as being glandular in nature: "In this instance we find that the glands of the body form the greater portion of such associations or activities. And, as we have indicated heretofore, one of the more sensitive glands to such is the thyroid, and the activities of same in their entirety." Apparently, a thyroid deficiency was contributing to the problem.

In this instance, Cayce's suggested regimen of treatment included internal medications to balance the activity of the thyroid, calcium supplements, and general spiritual advice. The individual was told that she could improve the condition by working with the physical recommendations and by seeking spiritual enlightenment and reading uplifting materials, such as that found in scripture.

Another case that involved the glandular systems of the body producing fear occurred in the case of an adult male who had come for a
reading in 1923. Fear, anxiety, and strained nerves were attributed to
lacerations on the lower portion of the stomach as well problems with
the adrenal glands. The individual also suffered from hypertension and
a shortness of breath. Cayce recommended internal medications, a phar-
macological remedy to soothe the intestinal tract, inhalants (apparently
for the shortness of breath), and electrical stimulation of the spine
(4790-1).

Even today individuals have found that recommendations given
years ago in the Edgar Cayce readings are still applicable in their own
experience. For example, a fifty-three-year-old woman came to me
seeking advice. She was troubled with frightening hallucinations. According to her story, it was her custom to meditate, pray, and reflect
over the day's activities in bed before going to sleep. One night a month
before coming to see me, she had begun to hear voices in her head just
outside of her ear. At first, she closed them off by thinking of other
things and even by getting up and moving around. The voices persisted. She began to realize that they were talking about her. She listened.

There were five different voices: two women and three men. They
seemed to be discussing the rearrangement of her nervous system so
that her body could be brought under complete control. Speaking as if
she was talking to real people, Miss Roberts ordered the voices to leave.
They stopped talking for a short time, then began again. Miss Roberts
told me that this frightening auditory hallucination had continued night
after night until she had begun to grow weak from lack of sleep. She
was afraid to tell anyone about her plight, fearing they would consider
her crazy. She had heard of the horrors of shock treatment, feared con-
finement, and had, she said, seriously considered suicide.

When I questioned her, Miss Roberts gave many of the details of the
conversations she was overhearing. She thought that when she spoke
the voices stopped. When they began again, they referred to her gradual
loss of control. Their general attitude was: "We will soon be able to
control her completely, including such automatic responses as breath-

ing and blood flow. We can even keep her from killing herself."

"They can make me move parts of my body now, even when I resist," Miss Roberts told me. "They can make me feel sensations I try not to experience."

From studying the Edgar Cayce readings for people who claimed to hear voices and from talking to many persons who believed they heard them, I was familiar with this kind of inner horror. In some physical diagnoses, Edgar Cayce described a third and fourth cervical lesion (irregularity) in the spine as being related to impaired functioning of the thyroid gland. I urged Miss Roberts to seek the assistance of an osteopathic physician who could make specific adjustments in the spinal area. At the same time, I suggested that she have a blood test that would indicate the level of the thyroid activity. As it turned out, the thyroid was deficient in its activity, and proper medication was administered. Miss Roberts stopped hearing the voices and they have not returned.

However, it should not be thought that a couple of osteopathic treatments and some thyroid extract were all that was involved to solve the problem. Miss Roberts later wrote:

> **I hope there will be an explanation of the full regimen of baths, steams, gentle massage, diet, violet ray [an electrical appliance designed to stimulate circulation], and, so important, the mental turnabout that had to be done—the constant battle to keep thoughts creative and constructive when part of my brain seemed totally unable to function. That fight back for me was hardest of all. Pushing through the deep and lonely lostness; the dark sense of separation from Him. It couldn't have been done without loving compassionate help from several people around me.**

The good news is that Miss Roberts was eventually able to function normally in life, carrying a normal workload, and is able to interact positively with dozens of people in her daily life. Is it possible that Miss Roberts very concrete fear pattern was produced by a specific physical condition? Any clinical psychologist or psychiatrist can give you a number of case histories of voices that produce frightening experiences. In my book, *Venture Inward*, I also included a number of such cases. Since then I have received accounts of many others. According to these stories, many of the experiences began when individuals started "playing with" automatic writing or Ouija boards. In the case of Miss Roberts, the physical condition of the thyroid and the spinal lesion—accompanied by some anemia, perhaps—seemed to have caused a leak from the unconscious that resulted in many terror-stricken nights and days until balance could be achieved.

Frequently, Edgar Cayce made reference to the spiritual centers of the body. These are associated with the seven endocrine glands of the body: gonads, cells of Leydig, adrenals, thymus, thyroid, pineal, and pituitary. They can also be referred to as the chakras—a Sanskrit word for "wheels," describing their appearance as pulsating vortexes of energy.

The readings attribute memory to each of these endocrine glands. Not only memories of repressed experiences, fears, and problems, but also memories associated with past-life experiences. Distortions of perception can certainly result if the glands of the body have been disturbed. Just as shadows become menacing forms for a frightened child, or a beautiful tree becomes a monster in the dark to a young Cub Scout, so the distorted perceptions brought on by faulty nerve coordination can lead us to mistake the normal sensations of our bodies and cell memories of our past perceptions for frightening specters that arouse not only specific fears but also confusing and crippling anxiety.

In summary, the cells of particular parts of our bodies can literally take on disturbed patterns, producing distorted perception resulting in fear and anxiety. As unsuspected functions of the endocrine glands are discovered and as we more and more recognize the effects of the mind on the physical body, we will be better able to deal with our fears. Edgar Cayce spoke on both of these concepts in the early 1900s. At the time, these ideas were new to the field of healing.

Suggestions for working with fears attributable to physical problems:

Taken together, the Edgar Cayce information on working with fears or anxieties due to a physical difficulty or problem often include recommendations such as the following:

1) Osteopathic or Chiropractic adjustments, oftentimes paying particular attention to the third cervical, ninth dorsal, coccyx, and sacral areas.
2) A physical check-up from an M.D., specifically looking for endocrine imbalance or dysfunction.
3) A balanced lifestyle that includes mild exercise, a well balanced-diet, and time for rest and relaxation.
4) Positive affirmations that can attune the body to a sense of peace and an awareness of the individual's connection to the divine.
5) Reading uplifting materials, such as scripture. The readings oftentimes recommended these verses specifically: John 14, 15, 16, and 17, and Deuteronomy 30.
6) Working with spiritual principles and ideals.
7) Massage and physiotherapies, designed to increase circulation and relaxation.
8) Prayer and meditation.
9) Using the imagination to visualize the body being healed, well, and calm.
10) Watching your dreams for helpful insights about your self, your body, your state of mind, and your relationship with God.

3

Repressed Fear Memories

Fear is the root of most of the ills of mankind, whether of self, or of what others think of self, or what self will appear to others.

5459-3

THE YOUNG man's face took on a horrible expression and he screamed at me, "You goddamn–son–of–a–bitch, where have you hidden him?" Then he hit me a couple of times with glancing blows to the head and shoulders. Fortunately, two good–sized, adult men were close by. They helped me hold him until the police arrived and took him away. During the scuffle, he poured out a constant stream of curses and filthy language.

This encounter had taken place in the hallway, just outside my office in Virginia Beach. The young man was a teacher who taught English in a western college. He and a friend had been living together as a gay couple. Years before I had spoken with both of them and even questioned them about their relationship. They were two fine people and shared a companionship, which in many ways seemed mutually helpful. The partner of the young man who had attacked me had become ill and had gone home to his parents. Unexpectedly and suddenly, he had died. The family had called me and asked me to tell the teacher about his partner's death.

When I first phoned the young teacher to tell him the news, he understandably became very upset. However, he somehow became convinced that I had hidden his friend and that I was trying to keep them apart. He had a nervous breakdown. Shortly after our communication, he broke into my home—apparently looking for his friend—and frightened my wife and son. After the break-in, he came to my office, where the struggle had occurred. After the incident in my office, I called his family. They decided to place him in a mental institution for treatment.

Even though the young man was in treatment, after that incident I began to think I saw him in hotel lobbies, airports, and on crowded city streets. Each time I thought I saw him somewhere in a crowd, I felt uncontrollable panic. After this happened several times, something even stranger occurred. All at once, when I thought I saw his face, his face would somehow transform into another face—a face that I didn't even recognize. This went on for a couple of months.

Because it continued to happen, I was determined to try and figure out whose face I was seeing or remembering. I practiced relaxing and thinking back through my childhood. It took days of repeated effort, but one day I remembered an incident. That incident contained the face I was seeing:

When I was about eight years old, a great uncle, who was a doctor, had taken his son and me on his rounds in a nearby mental hospital. During the day a patient had grabbed me by the shoulders, pulled me close to him, and put his face close to mine. As an eight-year-old, I was terrified. Before my great uncle could help me, the mental patient grimaced horribly, looking right in my face. I knew beyond any doubt that the face of the mental patient was the one I was remembering.

Thankfully, the young teacher who had attacked me responded to treatment and was eventually released. He got his life back together and went on to do graduate work. Extremely remorseful for what had happened, he wrote me apology after apology. When he was able, he returned some money that I had once loaned him. My speaking and travel schedule eventually took me to the city where he was living and working, and I asked him to introduce me at the public lecture I was giving. After that introduction, I no longer hallucinated about his or the mental patient's face again.

Apparently, the childhood experience with the mental patient had been filed away and forgotten in my subconscious. Somehow, the young teacher's attack had brought back my memory of the distorted face. Sheer terror and childhood panic had paralyzed me again and again until I was able to face it and remember the incident. Forgiveness and friendly interaction with the young teacher finally erased the remnants of that memory altogether.

With a little retrospection and memory, many individuals might be able to recall how individuals from the present remind them of experiences with people in the past. For example, a talented hypnotist who is a friend of mine tried to help a woman with a speech difficulty. However, he was unable to induce even a light hypnosis in the woman. Upon questioning, the woman admitted that the hypnotist reminded her of an uncle who had often disciplined her in childhood. As a result, she was unable to allow herself to relax around him.

Recently, a psychologist who had helped a prominent businessman with a fear connected to an incident in early childhood told me about a similar experience. Apparently, the business executive was scheduled to give a short after-dinner talk on ladies' night at the local Rotary Club. He was well prepared and had no difficulty speaking in public. On this occasion, however, he did feel a little tired. The businessman looked out over his audience and began his presentation. For a while, things went as he had planned. However, in the middle of his talk, the executive was somehow overcome. He became confused, started choking, dropped his notes, and was suddenly forced to sit back down. In spite of his best intentions, he was unable to continue. He had to excuse himself from finishing the presentation.

The next day the executive showed up at the psychologist's office. Under light hypnosis, he was able to recall the speaking experience from the night before and he suddenly realized that he had become flustered after looking at a particular woman in the audience. At the time, he had no conscious memory of meeting this woman previously and he had no idea who she was. However, under deeper hypnosis, the executive recalled a vivid childhood experience from the first grade that seemed to be the source of what had happened to him during the lecture.

The businessman suddenly remembered his first grade teacher—she looked very much like the woman he had seen at the Rotary Club dinner. He remembered an embarrassing experience from the first grade when his teacher had yelled at him in front of the entire class to "shut up and sit down!" Completely, embarrassed and humiliated at the time, he had done so. Now, years later, he had automatically responded in the same way when the woman's face from the Rotary Club dinner had apparently triggered that memory. His anxiety had been an automatic reaction, arising from this unconscious memory pattern.

The Edgar Cayce readings contain numerous references to early childhood experiences being the cause of anxiety-fear reactions. For example, parents of a three-year-old girl contacted Edgar Cayce for help with their daughter. Apparently the child had episodes of fear—her behavior becoming so extreme that it was far beyond normal childhood fears. Her fear patterns seemed to occur whenever she was around loud noises or voices, or if she was in any situation with the slightest degree of tension. The parents wanted to know how to help their daughter overcome her problem. They also wondered what had caused the fear in the first place. Cayce traced the problem to an experience that had occurred very early in the child's development.

According to the reading, as an infant the child had once been witness to an angry argument. Cayce stressed that even though the child had not been directly involved in the argument, "Not to the child—to someone else in the hearing of the child . . . " (143-2), the argument had caused her to fear the possibility of getting hurt whenever she was around loud or tense situations. The parents were told that the original incident had become even more anxiety provoking because of the activities of the child's own imagination. This was the source of their daughter's fear.

In terms of addressing the problem, the parents were told to begin working with presleep suggestions. In other words, as their daughter was in bed, just before falling to sleep, each night they were to take turns speaking softly to her, giving her gentle, soothing suggestions. Those suggestions might include statements such as the fact that the girl had nothing to fear, that her mother and father loved her and would take care of her, that she was in a very safe place, and that she could be quiet, joyful, and happy. This approach was to be used for three to five days and then left off for three to five days and then repeated. Cayce assured the couple that by doing this for simply two or three cycles, the fear would be removed.

On another occasion, during the course of a reading for a physical condition, a thirty-seven-year-old man asked about his fear of water. Apparently he was fearful of swimming in water over his head—so afraid that he even became fearful if he simply looked down into deep water from the edge of a pool. Cayce told him that the fear had developed because of a situation in his early childhood. Although not mentioned specifically, the problem was apparently a situation such as a near drowning. In order to overcome the incident, the readings recommended using suggestion (e.g., "I have nothing to fear, this water is safe") as well as simply forcing himself to get into progressively deeper water as a means of assuring himself that there was nothing to be afraid of. Cayce suggested that either approach might prove effective at discharging the fear from his subconscious memory (2772-4).

Sometimes childhood incidents can be far more crippling than the cases just cited. For example, I spoke with a young man in his twenties about his shyness. It was not difficult to discover that his inability to speak to a girl, much less even spend time with one, probably arose from early childhood experiences of several whippings administered by his father over "indiscretions" involving playing doctor with the little girl next door. Not only had the young man never experienced sexual intercourse but he had never been alone with a girl or had a serious date.

As he described his situation, he said that whenever he had even attempted a conversation with the opposite sex he was greeted with symptoms that came to him automatically: stammering, trembling, tight throat, red face, awkwardness, dry mouth, and so forth. All of these were symptoms of fear. By this time the young man was twenty-five years old. I encouraged him to seek professional counseling to recall, address, and then heal this issue that now presented a crippling fear in the present.

Oftentimes, rather than being healed, childhood problems can become even worse as individuals attempt to cope with them through various means of escape or suppression. An example along these lines came in 1943 when a forty-one-year-old man wrote Edgar Cayce to tell him of a lifelong problem with fear. His problem had eventually been diagnosed as a chronic neurosis. The individual described his situation, as follows: "I have suffered from a deep-rooted fear complex nearly all my life . . . This has also been confirmed by a prominent psychiatrist . . . I have suffered constant fear a great deal of the time and am naturally very anxious for an early reading." (5123-1)

During the course of the reading, Cayce suggested that a childhood problem with fear had become magnified because the individual frequently allowed himself to lose control over his own emotions. His emotional state had led to indulgences in foods and activities that had eventually caused problems within his body. In the language of the reading: " . . . the body is itself's own enemy" and problems with eliminations had "gradually brought on a complication of disorders through the mental reactions and the physical conditions."

In order to free himself of his condition, the individual was told that he had to completely change his mental attitude towards himself, his situation and individuals around him: "There must be the holding to some general creative energies, for the body will gain much more by trying and in helping someone else, rather than pitying or excusing or condemning things in others." Without this measure, the readings assured him that nothing else could ever provide permanent help. In addition to a complete change of attitude, he was encouraged to place some of his concerns elsewhere by constantly doing something to be of help and assistance to someone else. A change of diet and various physical therapies were also recommended.

Toward the end of the reading, Cayce stated that as the individual worked with this new way of thinking and he went out of his way to help others, he would overcome his fear and anxiety, as well as the self-indulgent behaviors that had been contributing to the problem.

All individuals have a wealth of unconscious childhood memories that can and still do affect them in the present. One of the most unique examples of a childhood memory that was awakened in the present came to my attention during my World War II experience. At the time, our special services company, which was attached to one of Patton's tank corps, was quartered in a partially destroyed French chateau near Metz. The Germans were reluctant to leave the forts in that area, so for a month we serviced troops in the area with music, books, and motion pictures. Because of my background and interest, there was time on the side for a little experimentation with subjects such as ESP and hypnosis.

During some of these experiments, I was working with an able hypnotist in our unit. In our company of 125 men, we had found three or four individuals who could go into a very deep trance state—a state in which these individuals had little or no memory of the events that transpired during the hypnotic session. On one occasion, a young GI, about eighteen years old, went under quickly and, after being regressed to his childhood, began to speak with his grandfather. He appeared to be speaking with someone we could not see. Suddenly he began to speak German and then switched to a language no one present could understand.

While he was under, I asked him to continue speaking in English and he obliged. He said that he was delighted to see his grandfather and stated that he had missed going on trips with him to Egypt and India. Since the conversation made little sense, we decided to awaken him and bring him out of the hypnotic state. Reluctantly, the young man followed our instructions. Upon awakening, he seemed disturbed and quickly left the room.

The following morning between 2 a.m. and 4 a.m., I was on guard duty. During that time the young man came to talk to me. He told me that his grandfather had died even before he had been born. However, when he had been about six years old, he began to dream each night that his grandfather came and took him to distant places, such as Egypt and India. On these "trips," they had observed "strange ceremonies." After repeatedly telling his family about these experiences, they became concerned. Not knowing what else to do, they took the young boy to a psychiatrist who hypnotized him and wiped out the memory of these dream experiences. Apparently, when he was once again under hypnosis, the childhood memories had been reawakened.

To be sure, that two–hour guard duty involved one of the most unusual conversations I have ever had. The young GI told me that he now recalled witnessing numerous experiences that were totally foreign to him. He described scenes of priestly initiation ceremonies that were completely unfamiliar. Because I had some knowledge of Tibetan and Egyptian mysticism at the time, I recognized some of his descriptions. After the war, I verified the young man's experiences as a child with his mother.

The GI went on to become an executive in a large corporation and has retained his knowledge of priestly rites and practices in both Tibet and Egypt—information that he has never consciously studied. Although it might be hard to rationally explain how these experiences had occurred, there is no doubt that they had remained locked inside his subconscious mind.

Another case involving early memory concerns a young man who, in a deep, relaxed reverie state, recalled a scar on the face of the doctor who delivered him. His mother later confirmed his memory.

Both conscious and unconscious anxiety–fear patterns of the mind may also be evoked in altered states of consciousness. Drug induced states of consciousness can produce states of confusion or ecstasy, feelings of deep depression or thoughts of wellbeing. Frequently, a self-induced drug state becomes the impetus for awakening anxiety–fear patterns that seem to reside within the body cell memory.

The following experience comes from an interview with a young man in his late twenties. He related how he had become acquainted with a man about his age that invited him to come over with a few others for drinks and marijuana. Eventually, the acquaintance offered to show him new states of awareness through a combination of drugs and hypnosis, promising to awaken his creative abilities in the process. The young man confessed to me that he soon became vaguely aware of the presence of danger. After each session with his new friend, he felt exhilarated and refreshed but this state of mind was soon replaced with one of fear and anxiety.

In spite of these feelings of anxiety, the young man discovered that he often felt motivated to go to his new acquaintance's apartment, even though he had no recollection of them having spoken of getting together. On each occasion, the so-called friend would simply smile and invite him in. He became fearful that the individual was trying to control his life. Eventually, the individual's face would seem to flash before his eyes at odd and various times, disturbing his work and personal life. He became convinced that he was losing control. At this point, he showed up in my office. I referred him to a good clinical psychologist, who helped him work through the problem and enabled him to break free of the experience.

A much more universal type of altered state of consciousness is sleep. Science has proven that we all dream much more than we remember. Every individual's dream life includes experiences of fear and anxiety. With this in mind, do our nightmares, our dreams of horror, or our dreams of losing control have anything to tell us about the causes of our fears? The Edgar Cayce material suggests that they do. One example concerns an eight-year-old boy who was having problems with fearful nightmares. The child briefly described one of those nightmares, as follows: "Mother and Daddy had left Brother and me alone at home. Brother was in the dark and holding a sponge in his hand that made a noise when moved through the air. I got scared of being in the dark . . . " (487-5)

The child's reading stated that the boy's deep-seated fear was being reflected in his nightmares. This fear was simply the fear of being left alone. In terms of how the fear had begun, Cayce stated that the fear had originated because the parents had oftentimes sent the child to his room and left him alone as a disciplinary measure, describing this punishment as being "for its own good." Because of the child's temperament and personality, this perception of abandonment had created excessive fear. The boy's parents were encouraged to use positive reinforcement rather than their previous mode of discipline. In other words, they were to encourage him whenever he did things that brought "joy, pleasure and happiness in the lives of others."

From the perspective of the Edgar Cayce readings, while individuals dream their mind can become open to deep states of consciousness and other levels of awareness. In addition to becoming aware of subconscious fears in the dream state, individuals often have psychic experiences and even experiences in altered states of awareness. For example, Cayce believed that real communication with a deceased loved one was not only possible in the dream state but was an experience that happened to most individuals who were watching their dreams. In one instance from the Cayce files a twenty-five-year-old woman was dreaming of her friend, Louis, who was deceased. According to the woman, during the dream she had told her friend, "If you really are Louis, pull me by the side." According to the woman, immediately she felt herself "pulled by the side in no uncertain manner and jumped up screaming in fear." (140-18)

Edgar Cayce explained to her that the experience had been a real encounter and that her subconscious mind had been in tune with the deceased individual. He assured her that this kind of encounter could be a natural occurrence and added that her fear of the unknown could prevent such an experience from occurring again.

As mentioned previously, the dream state can also open up an individual to psychic experiences and information. On one occasion, a college student described the following dream to me that had caused him to be afraid. He realized later that the dream had included a precognitive element:

> I had a very close childhood friend and we went on our separate ways in college; and when I returned home after having been in college for two years, we renewed our friendship. He was involved with drugs and emotional problems with his family. His mother was in an institution because of mental illness, and the father had deserted the family. He had been raised by his aunt. So he began to have psychological aftereffects from the drugs, and he became unbalanced to the point where he just couldn't hang out. So he was hospitalized in a mental institution; and, as a result of this, he never fully recovered, he just kept getting worse. He was taking massive doses of tranquilizers. But he went through several stages that are just classic. His mother was dying of cancer. He went with some relatives to see her for the final visit

in the hospital and bought a casket for her. So after she did die and they buried her, he returned to our hometown and disappeared for almost a week.

So I had a dream where I went to the door of his house and there were some children running around the house; and my father and I went to the back of the house to protect the back, and my brother and mother went to the front to protect the front of the house. We had sticks and we would wave them at the children and scare the children back. But then my friend appeared and we began to wrestle and fight, and I threw him on the ground and he pulled a pocketknife on me. He stabbed at me and I dodged him; I grabbed the knife, took it away from him, and put him down on the ground, told him that if he tried that again I would have to kill him.

I threw the knife away and I turned my back and was walking off. He picked up the knife and threw it at me, and it barely missed me. I took the knife, walked over to him and stabbed him.

Then I woke up from the dream, and it was horrible because I knew that I had killed him. Well, two days later I got a phone call saying that my friend had committed suicide. I knew in the experience that he was dead.

Obviously, the dreamer felt somewhat responsible for his friend and had wanted to protect him. His inability to help was responsible for the fear of somehow having "killed" his friend.

The following dreams imply that dreams can also be very effective in releasing, dealing with, and even healing suppressed fears. A young man in his twenties reported both dreams. They suggested that he had somehow found a way to face his fear and begin to work with it:

Dream 1—*I have been held captive by the devil for some time. At one point, when we are going outside at night with other hostages, I decide to try and escape.*

We are standing in a small, lighted area. I know if I can cross the area before the devil sees me, I will be able to escape into the darkness.

I take off running when I see that his is preoccupied with others. But as I run a voice tells me that if I continue I will risk falling into a well which is located in the darkness.

I stop, afraid to go on, but also afraid that he will see me. At this point, I see his shadow creep past me as I face the dark area, as if he is approaching from behind. In intense fear I pray, "Lord have mercy," and turn to face him.

But instead of the devil, I see a beautiful woman dressed in a white dress, surrounded with white light. She walks up to me and touches my forehead with her hand. The dream ends and I am aware that I have been healed.

Dream 2—*A black cat is irritating me. As I push it away, it comes back with renewed vigor. I grow afraid as the situation seems to be getting out of hand.*

But then I notice that I have what appears to be a lamp in my hand. I take a cover off of it and somehow activate it. The cat begins to cower in fear. As I prod it, it changes into a snake and scurries away.

A somewhat humorous example occurred in the case of a friend who told me about her daughter's frightening dream experience:

One night Christy was awakened, screaming and terrified. When I asked what was the matter, she said that she had been "dreaming of vampires."

"Vampires," I said, "you know there's no such thing as vampires."

"Yes," she answered, resolute through her sobs, "but there is such a thing as thinking about them!"

Perhaps surprisingly, our dreams can provide a means of dealing with fears and anxieties that we may consciously feel we don't have time to deal with in waking life. Many of us have become so accustomed to cultural pressures that we are unaware that common everyday mental patterns can be the sources of fear and anxiety. We often tend to push them out of consciousness, causing them to turn up in strange ways.

The preceding examples of fear patterns indicate that repressed fears can cause problems later on in life. Oftentimes, when a fear is released from the subconscious mind, individuals have difficulty staying focused on the present because their experiences from the past take over. The mind, functioning through the physical body, is the custodian of many fears and anxieties. These can be imagined difficulties that will never happen; suppressed early childhood traumas, all carefully recorded in the brains; primitive beliefs; suppressed sexual drives; implanted suggestions that may threaten to control life; conscious or unconscious cultural pressures; and, dreams that release suppressed fear patterns. Developing the ability to hold oneself in the present can often enable the individual to more adequately handle symptoms of fear as they arise. In this manner, the energy used to express anxiety can become transformed into constructive patterns of thought and action. When we turn later to the work of transforming anxiety and fear energies to more constructive expression, we will see what an important part the mind plays in this process.

Suggestions for working with repressed fears:

Taken together, the Edgar Cayce information on working with fears or anxieties due to a repressed childhood incident or problem often includes suggestions such as the following:

1) Working with a counselor or regression therapist to go back to the source of the fear pattern and attempting to deal with the situation from the perspective of adult, mature consciousness.

2) Talking with older relatives about possible childhood experiences that could have been the source of present-day fears.

3) Reviewing family history—perhaps prompted by looking through a photo album—to uncover possible tension experiences. Alternatively, you may decide to discuss experiences of tension with a close friend or companion.

4) Working with dreams can be a very effective measure, especially the process of recording dreams to look for sources of fear that may have been suppressed.

5) Working with presleep suggestion to overcome fear and anxiety. Much like biofeedback, either have a loved one give you the suggestions to overcome your fears as you begin to feel relaxed while drifting off to sleep, or record your own suggestions and listen to them as you lay down and relax.

6) A balanced lifestyle that includes mild exercise, a well balanced-diet, and time for rest and relaxation.

7) Positive affirmations that can attune the mind to a sense of peace and an awareness of the individual's connection to the divine.

8) Reading uplifting materials, such as Scripture. The readings oftentimes recommended these verses specifically: John 14, 15, 16, and 17, and Deuteronomy 30.

9) Working with spiritual principles and ideals.

10) Massage and physiotherapies, designed to increase circulation and relaxation.

11) Prayer and meditation.

12) Working with personal journals to dialogue with your fears.

4

Fears from Past-Life Memories

In the one before this we find in that land . . . known now as
Georgia . . . contempt was heaped upon the entity; though not at
fault, yet resentment was builded in the entity in his relationships
to others, and an air of fear is exhibited and builded in the present
experience. This must be overcome.   1720-1

CLOP—CLOP—clop! The wooden-soled shower slippers made a
rhythmic sound as the soldier came down the barracks aisle.
The time was 1942; the place, Fort George G. Mead between Bal-
timore and Washington, DC. My carbine was dismantled on my bed as
I cleaned each small part. I looked up at the naked figure, towel over
one arm, his soap clutched in one hand, as he came opposite my cot.
The man had dark hair and rather critical eyes, though the face appeared pleasant enough.

All at once everything faded. The scene changed and I could see that

I was in a desert place in front of a small fire. Two other teenaged boys sat across from me, wearing flowing white garments. (One of these individuals appeared to be the young man who was now standing in front of me.) Nearby, white racing camels were tied in place. In the distance, I could see other camels, with their riders approaching. Around the campfire, the three of us became terrified with fear.

Just as quickly as the scene had appeared, it faded from my mind and before I could catch myself I heard myself saying, "I haven't seen you since we were caught stealing camels in the Gobi Desert!" The young man stopped—looked at me intently for a moment, then went on to take his shower. It would be more than a year before the two of us worked up enough nerve to have a conversation about the experience.

What brought about that strange, uncontrollable sensation of fear—not of death, because I felt that we knew the riders who were approaching—but fear of a very severe beating? It all transpired in a matter of seconds, yet that scene has haunted me through the years.

Gina Cerminara, psychologist and author of a classic dealing with the subject of reincarnation, *Many Mansions*, used to say, "Psychology will take on an exciting new dimension as reincarnation is taken into consideration." With this in mind, the concept of rebirth does seem to be helpful in explaining some issues related to individual anxieties and fears. This is certainly the premise found in the Edgar Cayce readings.

As background information, Cayce believed that each individual is, in essence, a spiritual being, a soul. Cayce described the fact that the soul consists of three basic qualities—essentially described as mind, will and spirit. While in three dimensions, the soul enters a body that attracts it to and/or to which it is drawn because of choices made in previous lives. These choices and experiences remain a part of the soul mind's unconscious memory. From this perspective, a child is not a "new" soul—it only has a new body. The soul–called memory of the soul is really what most individuals refer to as "karma." Each individual has memories of talents and special interests, as well as weaknesses and negative emotional drives. The law of cause and effect is simply carried over from one life to another.

As a soul moves from one lifetime to another, it may change sex, race, and religion according to the way choice is exercised in relation to spiritual laws such as patience, faith, and love. Remember the real life of the soul is "other-dimensional." The soul did not begin in the earth; it will not end here. Three-dimensional life might be said to be a diversion from the real experience. The three-dimensional earth plane is neither a hell nor a prison, but rather a school, through which by the mercy and grace of God individuals can come to remember their true relationship with their Creator.

The following examples are taken from nearly 2,000 psychic discourses on past-life experiences from the Cayce files that came to be called "life readings." Rather than being the stuff of fantasy, these discourses provide psychological analyses, explanations of weaknesses and problems, as well as advice for vocational guidance and mental and spiritual growth. Many of these readings were requested by individuals who had been previously helped with physical advice; others were referred by a friend, who had found the information in his or her own life reading helpful, hopeful, and practical.

In 1929, Cayce told a thirty-seven-year-old man that his fear of positions of authority and power were traceable to a previous life in which he had misused power as a means of controlling others. In a Greek incarnation, he had been involved in a group overthrow of the government. As a reward for his participation, he had been placed in a position of authority himself. According to the reading, afterwards he lost "in the misapplication of aggrandizing self with power when others were put beneath the notice of the entity's efforts." (2467-1) Apparently, because of the way he treated others, he began to fear that they would seek revenge against him. That fear of the ramification of the misuse of power remained with him in the present.

In order to overcome this subconscious fear, the readings suggested that he attempt to conquer himself and his own desires. He was also to begin to see and understand that power was best used as a means of serving others rather than as a means of making others subservient to self. Cayce assured him that as he gained this awareness, his fear of positions of power and authority would begin to dissipate.

In 1931, a forty-five-year-old woman, Miss Young, sought information in a past-life reading. One of the woman's lifelong fears had been a fear of crowds and closed-in spaces. She had also once had the experience of becoming overcome with the same kind of fear while touring a cave. During the course of the reading, Cayce traced this fear to her most recent past life in early America, near Fredericksburg, Virginia.

During that lifetime while she was a young girl, Miss Young's home had been attacked and burned by Indians. Apparently, during the attack, the young woman and her family had barricaded themselves in the cellar, where they had smothered to death as the house burned down around them. In the language of the readings, "losing life in the experience by being crushed . . . this bring physical innate influence of crowds, or smothering feelings." (560-1)

Interestingly enough, after the reading was given the woman and her sister accompanied friends to the Fredericksburg area, looking for records of that previous life. The sister later described an agonizing experience that took place in a motel room on the outskirts of the city. During the night, Miss Young's labored breathing awakened her sister. Totally unconscious, the sleeping woman began to gasp for breath, turned red in the face, and threw herself off the bed onto the floor. The sister shook and struggled with her to no avail. Finally, the sister called the friends who were traveling with them. In desperation, they threw an ice pail full of water on her, and she woke up gasping and then began screaming.

Upon awakening, Miss Young had no memory of her dream experience. However, the sister wondered whether she had been reliving the smothering experience, recounted by Cayce, from a past life. It is possible to say, of course, that Miss Young may have taken the reading as factual and friends may have unconsciously dramatized the incident. Both women assured Edgar Cayce that all her life Miss Young had become panicky in crowds and close places, including elevators. After the motel incident, her claustrophobia began to diminish and eventually disappear.

In two cases dealing with the fear of sexual intimacy both women were told that their fear was the result of past-life experiences. One of the women was sixteen when her reading was obtained and the second was fifty-two. Although the problem had been traced to a past life in both cases, in each instance Cayce explained that the fear had developed from very different experiences.

In the first case, the eighteen-year-old woman was told that she had been raped in a previous life, and although she deeply desired male companionship she was intensely afraid of relationships because of that experience: "And these have brought, with the present experience, some fears that are *deep* in the innate experiences of the entity . . . " (768-4) In this instance, Cayce provided what might seem like an unusual curative approach. Because the rape had apparently occurred out of doors, she was encouraged to become active in outdoor games and various athletic sports. By participating in these activities, she would be able to overcome the fear that resided in her subconscious mind, as well as her physical body.

In the second case, the woman was a chiropractor. Although she definitely wanted to be loved in a personal relationship, she did not feel that anyone else would find her attractive or appealing. Making the problem even worse, she expressed a fear of close personal relationships with men to the point of almost being repulsed by them. In the beginning of her reading, Cayce reminded the woman that: "The individuality is the sum total of what the entity has done about those things that are creative or ideal in its varied experiences in the earth." With this in mind, he went on to explain that in one of her past lives she had taken the religious vows of "chastity, purity and devotion to celibacy." Because she had so created in her mind the idea that sex was to be completely avoided, this vow had remained deep within her subconscious memory.

When she asked, "How did the entity's inferiority complex originate?" Cayce replied, "For the fear or dislike of men. You cannot be one who took the vows and kept them and then lightly turn around and try to gratify the appetites of those who are not easily satisfied." To the question, "What have been the causes of so much fear in the entity's life?" the answer came, "Read just what has been indicated." In order to overcome the problem, her reading provided the following advice:

For the body is indeed the temple of the living God. Act like it! Keep it clean. Don't desecrate it ever, but keep it such that it may be the place where you would meet thine own better self, thine own God-self. As ye do this, there may be brought harmony,

peace, joy. As in everything else, if ye would have joy ye must
make others happy! Bring joy to others. If ye would have love, ye
must show thyself lovely! If ye would have friends, show thyself
friendly! If ye would know God, search for Him, for He is within
thine own self! And as ye express Him in the fruits of spirit; love,
grace, mercy, peace, longsuffering, patience, kindness, gentle-
ness; ye will find such within thyself. For if ye would have life
indeed (and life is the manifestation of God) ye must give it. For
the manner in which ye treat thy fellow man is the manner in
which ye treat thy Maker. This is the source of life, the source of
love, the source of peace, the source of harmony, and as ye give
expression to same, it may come indeed to thee.   4082-1

A thirty–six–year–old choir director who had an intense fear of sing-
ing in public was told that the fear had originated in France when she
had been persecuted for her beliefs. That persecution had created a
deep complex and fear regarding what other people would think of her.
When she asked, "How may this be overcome?" Cayce replied, in part:
"The trust that may be created in the inner self, through the associations
of self with that attained in many experiences, will overcome this." (1917-
1) In other words, positive experiences and positive reinforcement in
the present regarding her talents and abilities would enable her to eradi-
cate the fear from her subconscious mind.

In 1943, parents of a four–year–old girl brought their daughter to Mr.
Cayce for a reading in the hopes that it would enable her to overcome
a problem with fear and anxiety that had not been able to be diagnosed. The girl's mother described the situation, as follows:

She is vital, high strung and seems to have an excessive amount
of nervous energy. Sometimes, after sleeping in the afternoon,
she awakes in a lost, distraught frame of mind, rings her hands
and cries ceaselessly. It seems to be a sort of seizure or fit. I am
very quiet with her and in about a half-hour she becomes normal
again, and she doesn't seem to have any recollection of what
troubled her. I need much guidance in caring for and educating
her. I sent her to nursery school thinking that association with

other children would be beneficial for her. But she isn't happy
at school and I question whether I did the right thing . . .

Edgar Cayce traced the problem to a past life that had come to an
abrupt and sudden end just nine months prior to her birth in the
present experience. A small child at the time, apparently her family
home on the coast of France had been invaded and destroyed by the
German army. Cayce described the source of the fear, as well as what
had transpired in the previous lifetime, as follows:

> For, here we have a quick return—from fear, to fear through fear.
> And these bring, with those experiences of the entity, that which
> will require special influences to be put into the experiences of
> this mind; that it may be kept away from fear, away from loud
> noises, darkness, the scream of sirens, the shouts of individuals
> of fear to the entity.
>
> For, the entity was only just coming to that awareness of
> beauty of associations, of friendships, of the beautiful outdoors,
> nature, flowers, birds, and of God's manifestations to man of the
> beauty, of the oneness of purpose with individual activities in
> nature itself; and then the tramping of feet the shouts of arms,
> brought destructive forces. The entity then was only a year to two
> years older than in the present experience . . . The entity only
> passed out and then in less than nine months again entered a
> material world.   3162-1

In order to help the child overcome her fears, her parents were given
the following advice:

> Be patient. Do not scold. Do not speak harshly. Do not fret nor
> condemn the body-mind. But do tell it daily of the love that Jesus
> had for little children, of peace and harmony; never those stories
> such of the witch, never those as of fearfulness of any great
> punishment; but love, patience.

On various occasions in the Cayce files, every imaginable fear might be pinpointed as having its basis in a past-life experience. For example, parents of a two-year-old child, who possessed a very severe fear of an adult family friend, were told that during an Egyptian experience the family friend and the child had known each other. In that incarnation the present-day adult had somehow been responsible for the death of the two-year-old. Evidently a deep unconscious memory was the cause of the fear in the present (2148-7).

In another instance, a forty-six-year-old woman was told that her constant fears and anxieties related to asking herself, "What will people say?" and "What will be the ultimate outcome?" came as a result of a past life in England when she had been under almost constant scrutiny and criticism. Cayce informed her that this questioning and the fear related to it was constantly undermining herself: "These bring fear and trembling at times, and the entity fails through fear." (5424-1)

A thirty-eight-year-old woman was told that her fear of abandonment and homesickness was due to a previous existence when she had abandoned her own family, later deeply regretting her own actions (2401-l). A forty-seven-year-old man was told that his ability to provide counsel and advice to others was due to the fact he had once served in a similar position hundreds of years earlier to the king. Apparently, during that previous lifetime, his advice had not always been taken and he was often concerned regarding what the ruler might think of his thoughts and ideas. That experience had led to a fear of being censured by others in his current lifetime. Cayce informed him, "This should be better conquered in the present experience." (108-1) On another occasion, an eighteen-year-old was told that her fear of the dark was due to the fact that she had been confined in a dungeon during a French experience (852-12).

Similarly, when a fifty-four-year-old asked about the reason behind childhood fears of "animals, spiders, and sharp knives," Cayce said it was, "Because of those experiences when thou wert bound about, in those periods in France, when thine associates bound thee for thine virtue, and those activities in the knives, the racks of torture that were all about the entity." (823-1)

On another occasion, a woman who was afraid of water was told that the reason was because she had once been unjustly tried and "ducked" as a witch (1789–7). Another fear of water was discussed in the case of a twenty–nine–year–old woman who wondered how her daughter's fear of water could be overcome. Cayce traced the condition to a past life and stated that it could be healed with presleep suggestions, by telling the girl about all of the wonderful uses for water. Years later the mother, who stated that the approach had worked immediately, filed this report:

> **I'm very happy to say that thanks to my reading we were able to complete[ly] eliminate my daughter's [5043]'s, fear of water. We followed the instructions one night and the next day she was a changed child. Just loved the water after that and is an excellent swimmer now.**   **2428-1 Report File**

Oftentimes Cayce's approach for working with fears from past lives included regression, presleep suggestion, therapeutic counseling, physical therapies, positive affirmations, spiritual pursuits, and so forth.

In my own experience, a past–life problem presented itself in the form of a young man named William who had come to attend a conference in Virginia Beach, Virginia. During the course of the week, I had several opportunities to work with him because he stated that he wanted help in overcoming his fear. From the very beginning I could see that William was hesitant to really discuss his fears. To help him relax, I worked with him using various hypnotic reveries. During the course of one of those reveries, I asked William to tell me what he was afraid of. He tried to speak—dry lips moved and his words ran together. He choked a little, cleared his throat, and then managed to say only: "I don't know."

During the weeklong conference, I was able to repeat these hypnotic reverie sessions with him. Slowly, the story was revealed. Evidently, a childhood trauma had lodged in his subconscious and now at twenty-two had only partially broken through consciousness to distort his thoughts and actions. His father had caught him as a child with his young sister involved in sex play. The anger and violence that resulted engendered fear and antagonism toward his father, as well as a repressed determination to continue to be sexually attracted to his sister.

Over the years and well into adolescence his attraction to his sister had grown into what amounted to fascination. He had become jealous of his father's relationship with his sister because the relationship seemed to have its own element of sexual attraction. In time, his mother was drawn into the situation, causing volatile and angry arguments. Eventually, his parents divorced. Afterwards, the young man briefly attended a local college, where he became accustomed to smoking marijuana daily. His grades suffered, and he dropped out of school.

His fascination with his sister continued, but he was crippled by fear whenever he even spoke to any other girl. At twenty-two, William had never dated or experienced sexual intercourse. In fact, when we first spoke it was difficult for him to look another person in the eye. His head hung down and his words often tumbled out incoherently.

Could there possible be something deeper to this situation than the childhood experience William had recalled? The boy's fascination and the father's attraction for the same girl raised questions in my mind about a possible past-life memory. The young man's emotions were very strong. The attraction of both men had persisted.

I worked with William for the rest of the week and continued the light reverie technique we had used for recalling details of childhood incidents. One day, after several sessions, he completely relaxed and seemed less hesitant to follow the suggestions. I told him to imagine that he was walking down a quiet shady street and was entering a small, empty theater. Sitting quietly alone in the empty theater, he was to see the curtain open and describe the scene.

"There is a man in a small empty house. He's very sad, very sad. His wife has left him," William told me haltingly. The depth of his sadness was genuine. Further description of the scene brought the information that there had also been two small children and that the wife had run away with another man. He felt that he was the man in the small house. In addition, he felt that his sister in the present had been his wife from that experience.

Could there have been a past-life memory pushing the child, the adolescent, the young adult toward the sexual relationship with his sister, in spite of moral taboos and his father's anger? It did not take a vivid imagination to theorize that William's present-day father had been that other man.

In any event, talking about the situation and his praying for his sister and father began to clear up the crippling fear he had of contact with other girls. After our sessions and his return home, he wrote me to say, "I've had my first date. It wasn't too bad, but I was scared." Other dates have followed, and friends who know William report that he now looks people in the eye, smiles, and is beginning to talk more easily with those around him. He may have a hard road ahead, but he appears to be on his way.

Regardless of an individual's belief in reincarnation, this kind of re-gression therapy has been found helpful in assisting individuals at over-coming lifelong fears, deep-seated traumas, and unconscious blocks. It's also important to remember that even if a fear has its basis in a past life, these past-life fears are often fostered and enhanced due to present life experience as well as to the activities of the individual's mind.

Just as we are the sum total of all that we've experienced in this life, we are the total composite of all of previous experiences. Evidently, as our five senses begin to function, we put a protective covering over negative and positive soul memories. Only our strongest urges, good and bad, come through as patterns, which are generally emotional. Per-haps we are more complex than we know. Perhaps these memories from the past play a little understood but very important influence in our present lives. Perhaps even more important is the fact that through understanding the causes of our problems and accepting responsibility, we can begin to transform our negative patterns, including fears, into constructive, positive action.

Suggestions for working with fears from past lives:

Taken together, the Edgar Cayce information on working with fears or anxieties due to a previous lifetime often include the following rec-ommendations:

1) Working with a counselor or regression therapist to go back to the source of the fear pattern and attempting to deal with the situation from the perspective of present-day, adult, mature con-sciousness.

2) Working with personal inventories, reveries, and regressions in

an attempt to get to the source of a past-life problem. One example of a personal inventory can be found in Appendix B: "Bringing All Things to Your Remembrance."

3) Exploring historical places, music, or stories that might enable you to get in touch with previous life experiences and memories. Suggestions might include visiting museums and exhibits, paying close attention to your attractions and aversions to cultures and various periods in history.

4) Working with and recording your dreams can be very helpful at unlocking memories from previous lives.

5) Presleep suggestion was often recommended as a way to overcome fear and anxiety.

6) A balanced lifestyle that includes mild exercise, a well balanced-diet, and time for rest and relaxation.

7) Positive affirmations that can attune the mind to a sense of peace and an awareness of the individual's connection to the divine.

8) Reading uplifting materials, such as Scripture. The readings oftentimes recommended these verses specifically: John 14, 15, 16, and 17, and Deuteronomy 30.

9) Working with spiritual principles and ideals.

10) Massage and physiotherapies, designed to increase circulation and relaxation.

11) Prayer and meditation.

12) Working with personal journals to dialogue with your fears.

13) You may also wish to become familiar with the many books that explore the topic of reincarnation; *Children's Past Lives*, by Carol Bowman, and *Twenty Cases Suggestive of Reincarnation*, by Ian Stevenson, M.D., are just two books that individuals have found helpful in exploring the subject of reincarnation on their own.

5

The Fear of Death

It is the fear of the unknown that first makes fear. 1776-1

IT WAS noontime. As the massage therapist began the final long, relaxing strokes along my spine, my wrist and upper part of my left arm began to ache severely. The pain continued as I dressed. I mentioned it to the therapist and he called the nurse on duty to take my blood pressure. It registered 190/98. Assuming that this unusually high reading had been brought on by the massage, I promised to have it checked later that day. I went for a short walk before trying to meditate. During meditation the ache moved to a different location—it filled my entire chest. It was then that I realized I was having a heart attack. At any moment my heart could stop. Quietly, Death sat beside me.

Immediately, I was taken to the hospital. Apparently, a mild heart attack continued as an electrocardiogram was taken. For the next three days, I did not move without assistance.

In one long, quiet, sleepless night, I asked myself the question, "Am I afraid of dying?"

Actually, several questions entered my mind: "Will pain be involved?" "Am I going to be punished?" "Is there a God out there?" "Has He gone away and left us in this crazy world?" Suddenly, my war experience that had prompted some of the very same questions came clearly back to me.

Thankfully, because of the well-publicized work by pioneers such as Elisabeth Kübler-Ross, M.D., author of *On Death and Dying*, and Raymond A. Moody, Jr., M.D., author of *Life After Life*, the subject of death and dying has become more openly discussed. Nevertheless, for countless people, the topic of death remains a great unknown or a least a subject to be avoided.

During one of my nights in the special cardiac care unit, I actually heard a woman die. She cried out, "Won't somebody help me? Please, somebody help me." The call probably came not as a result of pain but perhaps because the first darkness of losing physical consciousness had begun. There was a rushing of nurses, a call for the doctors, followed by hurried calls to members of her family. Very early in the morning, her body was rolled past my open door.

Unless we are in a war zone, trapped in a catastrophe of some kind, or work in the field of medicine, most of us seldom come that close to the presence of death. Perhaps it is time for humankind to begin seeing death as a friend, rather than some terror or ghostly figure from childhood meant to frighten young people in movies or on Halloween. In fact, as we become aware of our relationship to the oneness of all Force, our own death ceases to be all that important.

On a number of occasions during his forty-three years of psychic work, Edgar Cayce recalled a variety of dreamlike experiences that occurred just before, during, or just at the close of one of his readings. In one of these experiences he met the personification of death. Upon awakening from his trance state, he described the encounter, as follows:

> **I was preparing to give a reading. As I went out, I realized that I had contacted Death, as a personality, as an individual, or as a being. Realizing this, I remarked to Death: "You are not as**

ordinarily pictured—with a black mask or hood, or as a skeleton, or like Father Time with a sickle. Instead, you are fair, rose-cheeked, robust—and you have a pair of shears or scissors." In fact, I had to look twice at the feet or limbs, or even at the body, to see it take shape.

He replied: "Yes, Death is not what many seem to think. It is not the horrible thing which is often pictured. Just a change—just a visit. The shears or scissors are indeed the implements most representative of life and death to man. These indeed, unite by dividing—and divide by uniting. The cord does not, as usually thought, extend from the center—but is broken, from the head, the forehead—that soft portion we see pulsate in the infant. Hence we see old people, unbeknowing to themselves, gain strength from youth by kissing there; and youth gains wisdom by such kisses.

Indeed the vibrations may be raised to such an extent as to rekindle or re-connect the cord, even as the Master did with the son of the widow of Nain. For He did not take him by the hand (which was bound to the body as was the custom of the day), but rather stroked him on the head—and the body took life of Life itself! So, you see, the silver cord may be broken—but vibration . . . " Here the dream ended.   294-114 Report File

As individuals begin to examine and work with their fears, they can transform and heal them—even those fears related to death. Edgar Cayce called the transition between the physical state and death "God's other door," suggesting that death is simply a transitional state between levels of consciousness. Even as a young man, I had an experience with death that suggested this same continuity of consciousness.

It was 1927 and I was a freshman at Washington and Lee University in Virginia. Oftentimes, during that period, I found that I was having a difficult time explaining what my father, Edgar Cayce, did for a living. One sophomore named Gus Elias seemed to take particular delight in ribbing me about my father "being a psychic," and asking questions that I did not know how to answer. One afternoon, I remember that we had a fairly heated argument about the field of psychical research. Later that night, Gus had gone off to a dance near Natural Bridge, a nearby resort, and I had gone back to the dormitory to study and sleep.

Before daybreak, in the early hours of the morning I was suddenly awakened. I sat up in bed and soon realized that in spite of the fact that I was sitting, I could still see my body lying on the bed. Apparently, I was having what would later be known as an "out-of-body experience." I quickly discovered that I could move away from my body in consciousness and return to enter it at will. Although I had read that it was necessary to enter the body through one of the holes in it (mouth, nose, etc.), for me, that did not prove to be the case. My consciousness, the real me, seemed to be free of the body. Fascinated by what was occurring, I willed myself to move to the molding around the top edge of the room. I found that it was covered with dust.

Suddenly, the room began to fill up with a light-colored cloud. This cloud seemed to move in from the ceiling. To escape from it, I moved to the floor in the middle of the room. My body continued to be in bed asleep. In fact, I became conscious of the fact that I could hear my "other self" snoring.

All at once, out of the cloud came Gus Elias' voice and I could see his outstretched hand. "Cayce, come up here," he said, "this is terrific. I have to show you. Come up here!"

I tried to move toward the cloud but the hand was withdrawn. As the cloud touched what I call my consciousness, I became afraid. Immediately, I was back in my sleeping body. The cloud vanished. My body felt like a cold, clammy boot left outside on a camping trip. Physical consciousness returned. I quickly sat up, fully awake.

What sort of crazy dream had I just experienced? As I turned on the light to look at the clock, I could see that it was 2 a.m. At that same moment, someone began pounding on my door and calling, "Cayce, get up! Get over to the hospital. They are bringing Gus Elias' body in. He was killed at midnight." Gus had died in an automobile accident that very night.

Over the years, I have repeatedly spoken with people who claim to have had similar out-of-body experiences, not all associated with near-death. For example, after I had given a lecture in Sacramento, California, a mother and daughter relayed the following experience:

My daughter had just had her first baby. She and her husband
were living in Oregon. My son-in-law's mother was with them for
the birth of the child. I had not yet seen the baby but naturally
wanted to. One afternoon, still wearing my apron, I lay down for
a moment's rest. Almost instantaneously I seemed to be in my
daughter's home, where I had never visited. My daughter and her
husband were sitting on the couch in the living room. He was
holding the baby. As I stood in the doorway, they both looked up
and saw me. They seemed frightened. Suddenly, a ringing phone
awakened me. My daughter was on the other end, calling me long
distance because she was worried about me. She told me that
both she and my son-in-law had just seen me standing in the
doorway.

The daughter stood listening as her mother related the story and
added, "She was wearing her best dress." After making notes on the
story, I asked if I could call the husband (who was in Oregon) to confirm
their account. I immediately made the call and he confirmed what the
two had said without prompting.

What this suggests is that many out-of-body psychic experiences on
record demonstrate that it is possible to leave the physical body at will,
not just during the death experience. Fascinating questions arise because of these types of experiences. Although it might be assumed that
some of these experiences have been told and retold so often that "a
coincidence" becomes a phenomenon, many of them stand up under
close scrutiny. In the case of the woman and her daughter at the conference, the husband and wife had both seen the younger woman's mother.
The sleeping mother had seen her daughter, her son-in-law, and her
new grandchild. All three individuals had perceived the incident. Somehow time and space had collapsed.

According to Edgar Cayce, out-of-body experiences are more common than we realize. Oftentimes, these experiences occur naturally in
our dreams. A forty-three-year-old lawyer who had sought Cayce's advice on a number of occasions asked about the authenticity of his own
out-of-body experiences:

(Q) Do I actually leave my body at times, as has been indicated,
and go to different places?
(A) You do.
(Q) For what purpose, and how can I develop and use this power
constructively?
(A) Just as has been given as to how to enter into meditation. Each
and every soul leaves the body as it rests in sleep.

As to how this may be used constructively—this would be like
answering how could one use one's voice for constructive
purposes. It is of a same or of a similar import, you see; that is,
it is a faculty, it is an experience, it is a development of the self
as related to spiritual things, material things, mental things.

                                                            853-8

In January 1953, Thomas Sugrue, author of the Cayce biography *There
Is a River*, and a long-time friend, was critically ill in a New York hospital
following an operation on his knee and hip. I wanted to see him before
his death and made arrangements to go to New York. Before the trip,
however, I had the following dream:

I was in the New York hospital and on the floor where I seemed
to know that Tom Sugrue had a room. When I entered the room,
he was sleeping and someone was with him. He awakened—not
physically but a part of his consciousness. Even though his
physical body remained asleep in bed, another part of him got up
from the bed and walked with me to a small waiting room on the
floor. He explained that he was going to die and that there was
no need for me to come to see him. Under the circumstances, he
stated that such a contact would mean little to his physical
consciousness. We talked about Edgar Cayce's work. He said that
in spite of his death he would continue to help. I knew that he
would.

Later, when I awakened and thought about the dream, I realized that
my dream body was just like the one I saw of Tom Sugrue getting up
from the bed and walking with me to the waiting room. It was like the

one I had seen when I was a young student and had during the experience with Gus Elias in my dorm room. In both instances, my body had
the general form of a physical body, yet you could see through it and it
moved easily through matter. Obviously, there is a part of us that functions independent of the physical body.

There is a vast amount of literature dealing with the survival of bodily
death. Therefore, any individual who has a fear of death should consider looking into some of the information for him or her self. Exploring
such material may lead to being released from a lifelong fear.

In the Cayce files on dreams and dream interpretation, there are literally dozens of cases in which individuals had possible communication with the deceased while dreaming. In fact, as early as 1923, Edgar
Cayce said in one reading, "...there is not sufficient credence given to
dreams; for the best development of the human family is to give the
greater increase in knowledge of the subconscious, soul or spirit world."
(3744-4)

During his unconscious state, while given readings, Edgar Cayce
sometimes had dreamlike experiences in which he encountered deceased relatives and friends, apparently verifying the possibility of communicating with those who are deceased as well as confirming the
survival of personality. While giving a reading on one occasion, Cayce
seemed to be speaking with my uncle, my mother's brother, who had
been dead for a number of years. My uncle described his activities and
indicated that members of the family would be waiting to greet my
mother when it came her time to die. He spoke of the house their grandfather had "built" on the other side—a place that had become a gather-
ing spot for various family members, who had also died.

"We are on that plane," my uncle went on, "where you have heard it
spoken of that the body, the mind, are one with those things we have
builded." (5756-13)

Cayce told one woman who had dreamed of communicating with
her mother, "Your mother is alive and happy . . . for there is no death,
only the transition from the physical to the spiritual plane. Then, as the
birth into the physical is given as the time of the new life, just so, then,
in physical is the birth into the spiritual." (136-33) On another occasion
when speaking about death, Cayce told a group: "[One is] Free of the

material body but not free of matter; only changed in form as to matter; and is just as acute to the realms of consciousness as in the physical or material or carnal body, or more so." (262–86)

A great many people asked Edgar Cayce about personal experiences related to death that were not simply dreams. Some confirm material that is given in the dream readings. In 1935, a fifty–seven–year–old woman, whose letters mentioned her interest in metaphysical subjects, asked a question about one of her experiences. The answer she received suggests that after death there is the process of a continual growth in consciousness:

> **(Q) In regard to my first projection of myself into the astral plane, about two weeks ago: Some of the people were animated and some seemed like waxen images of themselves. What made the difference?**
>
> **(A) Some—those that appear as images—are the expressions or shells or the body of an individual that has been left when its soul self has projected on, and has not been as yet dissolved—as it were—to the realm of that activity.**
>
> **For what individuals are lives on and takes form in that termed by others as the astral body. The soul leaves same, and it appears as seen. Other individuals, as experienced, are in their *animated* form through their own sphere of experience at the present.**
>
> **(Q) Why did I see my father and his two brothers as young men, although I knew them when they were white-haired?**
>
> **(A) They are growing, as it were, upon the eternal plane. For, as may be experienced in every entity, a death is a birth. And those that are growing then appear in their growing state.   516-4**

Her remark about "waxen images" as "shells" suggests to me that the soul, after a time, leaves this shell, just as we leave the flesh body at death.

In 1943, a fifty–seven–year–old man came to Edgar Cayce because of a serious health problem. His physical body was experiencing problems with the liver, poor circulation, an ongoing strain on the heart, and severe hypertension. The situation was described as being "rather serious." Nonetheless, the man eventually wrote and explained how being so close to death had actually enabled him to overcome his fear of it:

> About 2 weeks ago I had 3 very severe hemorrhages outward but nevertheless I went down close to death . . . When I was laying flat on my back in the valley of shadows, I noted one thing, the closer I was to parting from this world, the less I feared it, and the calmer my mind was. My body was making a hard struggle, my heart seemed to stop beating for a definite time, and when breathing came again, it was a long drawn breath. Then after a period of time my heart beat rapidly, pounded so, and my breath in gasps, yet my mind was calm, and I think clear. Now I don't think I ever will fear that breaking of earthly ties in the future, nor will I ever dread it. Not that in the past I spent a lot of time in morbid contemplation and fear of it but I nevertheless did have some dread of the experience.   3443-1 Report File

Keeping in mind that the readings warned against the act of suicide, during the course of a reading given to a twenty–eight–year–old naval officer, Cayce suggested that death could be a positive experience when it occurred as a natural part of the cycle of life:

> The death is separation, and thus man hath dreaded same; yet when it has lain aside its phase that maketh afraid, it is but the birth into *opportunities* that—if they are embraced with Him, the *truth, as* thy guide—will bring joy and harmony into thy experience!   1776-1

When my wife became pregnant with our first child, her brother, a medical doctor, told me that we might expect a difficult birth and recommended that we consult a specialist. As a result, we obtained the services of a specialist. Because my father was still alive at the time, I obtained a reading on my wife's condition. Cayce also indicated that it would be a difficult birth. Both individuals proved to be correct. Had it not been for the foreknowledge and intervention of the doctor, we could have lost both my wife and my son.

As a result, I was hesitant to have another child. However, my wife was less concerned than I was, so we decided to have a second child. This happened after the war and after both my mother and Edgar Cayce were deceased. As the delivery time drew near, I found that I was more and more concerned about my wife's situation.

One night, I had just come home from giving a lecture and went into our bedroom. My wife was asleep, and a small light was on in the hallway. I sat on the edge of the bed and prayed that both she and the baby would be okay.

Suddenly, a light went on in the corner of the room. Contained within the light I could clearly see the smiling faces of both my mother and father. In my head, I could hear my father's voice: "Hugh Lynn, you shouldn't worry. It's going to be all right. We are going to show you what love can do."

All at once the light and their faces moved toward me. As the light touched my body, I lost physical consciousness, but became aware of the presence of both my mother and father—somehow in me. Then there was a pull and all three of us where in the sleeping body of my wife. I became aware of the presence of my wife and of the unborn child, as well as of my father, my mother and myself. The joy and ecstasy I experienced in those few moments was beyond description.

All at once there was another pull and we were back in my body. Suddenly there was a click and the faces of my parents were again in the corner of the room in the light. My mother was smiling and I heard my father's voice once more: "You see what love can do? It's going to be all right. You are going to have a son. Stop worrying." Then the light went out.

I sat there on the bed crying. Joy, peace, love flooded through me. My wife woke up, turned over and squeezed my hand hard. Before I could say a word, she spoke: "Hugh Lynn, I've had a beautiful dream of your father and mother. It's going to be all right. We are going to have a boy."

When my wife finally delivered the baby, we did have a boy. Amazingly, the delivery came quite easy.

I am convinced that I communicated with both Gertrude and Edgar Cayce. For me, there is survival after bodily death. Death is something that we will all encounter. It is a transition that all of us most go through.

Perhaps death is simply another state of consciousness. A state that is alluded to in the New Testament with the words: "Let not your heart be troubled; ye believe in God, believe also in me. In my Father's house are many mansions." (John 14:1–2)

Rather than being frightened by the concept of death, we must find a way to awaken the spiritual part of us to a new sense of reality. The possibility that death is much like the state in which we find ourselves in our dreams and that we are in a process of growth and development that entails returning to the earth again and again, suggests that there is much more to the process of life and death than we may have been aware of. By awakening to that spiritual part of our selves, we may come to know that there is much more to us than we may have previously imagined and in the process we may see that we have the ability to transform many of our fears.

Suggestions for working with a fear of death:

Taken together, the Edgar Cayce information on working with fears or anxieties about death and the survival of individuality after death suggests that recommendations such as the following might be helpful:

1) Become familiar with books and materials that explore what the transition called death may be all about. In addition to summaries about the death experience by individuals such as Raymond Moody and Elizabeth Kübler Ross, you may also wish to read survival stories by people like George G. Ritchie, M.D., and others.

2) Explore other books that investigate what "God's other door" may be like; possibilities include: *Testimony of Light*, by Helen Greaves; *The Place We Call Home*, by Robert Grant; and, *The Boy Who Saw True*, by an anonymous author.

3) Begin working with your dreams to see how consciousness is not limited to the confines of a physical body. You may also begin to recall out–of–body experiences that occur in the dream state.

4) Reading uplifting materials, such as Scripture. In addition to frequently recommended verses like: John 14, 15, 16, and 17, and Deuteronomy 30, Psalms 23 and 100 may also be helpful.

5) Work with prayer, meditation, and activities designed to enhance your spiritual growth, faith, and belief in a Higher Power.

6

Reexamining Your Fears and Anxieties

Hence the need is only to be rid of fear itself. For, fear—to be sure—reacts upon this body in those ways as indicated, to produce pathological—from psychological—reactions.   2441-1

THE EDGAR Cayce readings suggest that one of the main reasons individuals experience failure in life is because they fail to heal longstanding patterns of fears. As just one example, when a thirty-one-year-old Jewish stockbroker asked in a reading why individuals so often failed at accomplishing what they knew or what they understood to do, Cayce gave the answer in one word: "Fear." (900-306) Rather than continuing to be fearful, anxious, disappointed, or discouraged by life's experiences and/or an individual's apparent problems, the readings suggest that by exploring, dealing with, and then healing these fear patterns, individuals will find that their lives can become much more constructive, more joyful and more fulfilling. With this goal in mind, obviously individuals may need to reexamine and come to some understanding of the source of their fears in the first place.

If your body is the source of fear patterns, you may have been receiving various signals in terms of physical incoordination, pain, tension, or slight malfunctions that could be alerting you to the existence of a problem at this level. Along these lines, do you have vague feelings of uneasiness? Are you under tension, easily irritated, or do you worry excessively over very small details? Is it difficult for you to relax, or are you waking up frequently and unable to get a good night's sleep? Are you oversensitive? Do you have small, constant, physical irritants such as dizziness or persistent headaches? Are your dreams nightmarish in quality? Do your dreams contain images of ill-kept houses—rotten underpinnings, faulty plumbing, or flickering lights? Do you dream of being in cars with poor brakes, malfunctioning motors, or are you going backward or driving erratically on bad roads?

Your unconscious may be giving you warning signals about a physical problem or situation. Anxieties can be the source of physical illness and, conversely, physical conditions can cause fear and anxiety. In terms of physical health and wellbeing, from the perspective of the Edgar Cayce readings the functioning, health, and balance of the nervous system and the endocrine glands are also an extremely important consideration.

Another source of many subconscious fears and anxieties can be found in childhood. From this standpoint, you may wish to examine your childhood memories, experiences and feelings. Where you somehow "programmed" as a child in ways that continue to affect you adversely in the present? Were you ever made to feel guilty by an overzealous parent, relative, or teacher? Was there an incident of misbehavior, stealing, or a childhood act of sex play that continues to affect you even now? If so, one of the first steps in addressing the issue may be to forgive your self for what took place in the past. Oftentimes, self must be forgiven first before self can forgive others. Seeing these childhood issues and experiences from the viewpoint of adult consciousness can also be a very effective part of personal therapy. Repressed guilt will continue to breed fear.

If your childhood memories do contain fear patterns that remain with you then you may need to explore these memories further. If these memories remain repressed, they can continue to affect you. All of us tend to push unpleasant experiences out of the mind. Look for periods in your childhood when a particularly fear-laden experience occurred, such as a repeated nightmare, a serious argument or confrontation, an accident or traumatic experience. Perhaps parents, siblings, aunts, uncles, grandparents, or friends can help you recall these periods of trauma and tension. Pay special attention to reports or memories of continued conditioning by parents or associates in which you might have frequently heard about the possibility of dangers or harm from certain people or activities.

Your mind is far more powerful than you may have ever realized. The readings are adamant in their statement that "mind is the builder." What you think about repeatedly, you build into the physical structure of your body—you become what you think. You are literally affected by what you believe. In order to address this dynamic, the mind must be disconnected from continually repeating negative thought patterns. Cayce put it this way on one occasion: "For just as hate and animosity and hard saying create poisons in the body, so do they weaken and wreck the mind of those who indulge in same. And then they begin to wonder *why* this or that has befallen them." (1315-10)

In another reading, we can find this statement: "No one can hate his neighbor and not have stomach or liver trouble. No one can be jealous and allow the anger of same and not have upset digestion or a heart disorder." (4021-1). The findings of psychosomatic medicine have confirmed this same point of view. For that reason, one important step in dealing with fear is the act of beginning to control one's mind and her or his thought processes.

Childhood can be the source of many conditioned fears or traumatic experiences suffered and forgotten that become the source of crippling memories, frequently attached to unreasonable childhood guilt. Adult reason allows us to laugh at some immature attitudes; but the unconscious memory can suddenly break through to the involuntary nerve control centers and reduce a person to a quivering, breathless, sweaty mass of flesh. Oftentimes, personal freedom begins with understanding the origin of the mind-body trauma.

Another important consideration in examining fears is the possibility that they are connected to previous life experiences and trauma. Each individual is the sum total of all of his or her memories, patterns, and experiences from past lives. Some of these patterns and experiences have assisted you throughout your life; others, perhaps, have been the root cause of fears and anxieties that may not appear to have any basis in your present experience. Each of us is very different from other members of our families—reincarnation can help to explain, in part, those differences. It is important to know that even if your fear can be traced to a past-life experience, you do not have to keep reliving this pattern as a source of fear and anxiety in the present; all fear patterns can become transformed.

As you begin to reexamine your fears, you may also need to examine your attitude toward God, death, and the unknown. How do you personally relate to a Higher Being, the Source of all life? Would you say that you are cooperating with or fighting against whatever you imagine to be God? Sometimes guilt, born out of a religious heritage or perhaps deep-seated in human memory patterns, can continue to haunt us. Whether this fear is born out of a childhood concern of "burning in hell" or the "meaninglessness of life," it may well stem from our separation from God, or a rebellion against Divine Will. Sometimes individuals wrestle with their lower human nature when they have lost contact with their concept of God. If you have been searching for a loving God whose plan you have not yet been able to fathom when weighed against the chaos occurring in today's world, you may be wrestling with fear in one of its most disturbing guises. Fears related to death and dying often take root because of this very issue.

Frequently, fears related to death and dying can also have their origin in questions regarding the survival of personality. On other occasions, these fears can be traced to worries about abandonment and isolation. There is a wealth of evidence and a variety of books available that detail the survival of personality, the continuity of the soul, and the incredible, loving experiences individuals encounter from an all-loving Creator during the death process. With this in mind, individuals with a fear of death have much helpful information available for their own personal exploration and enlightenment.

In summary, if you wish to begin exploring the source of fears and anxieties, you can begin by working with personal introspection and reflection. Answers to questions like these may be a first start, eventually enabling you to not only get to the root of the problem but also heal it so that you can become all that you were meant to be:

1. Is your body breaking down?
2. Do you have any childhood traumas that are still affecting you?
3. Are you being impacted by experiences from your own past lives?
4. What is it about death and dying that frightens you?
5. How do you think you and God are getting along?

For further insight into these same issues, enabling you to discover possible causes for personal fears, you may wish to complete the questionnaire in Appendix A: "Fear Questionnaire: Getting in Touch with Possible Causes for Personal Fears."

As you begin to know yourself better and grapple with fear patterns that have occurred in your own life, you may discover that the knowledge and the desire that you need to change may be some of the most important steps. The suggestions in this book are designed not for the seriously ill—those who may require serious, professional help—but rather for average individuals. Those who need additional assistance are encouraged to pursue the help of a counselor, a psychologist, a psychiatrist, a trained hypnotherapist, a knowledgeable minister, or a dedicated social worker. We are never really alone in the world. Whatever fear you may be struggling with, know that thousands before you have grappled with the very same problem. First work with your self, then choose to seek outside assistance if you need it.

7

Bringing Your Life into Alignment– Spiritually

There is the care of the Maker for that created. There is the duty of the created to the Creator. There is the love for the Creator of that created. There is that of the honor due the Creator by that created. The will of the one must become the will of the other, and in that may be found the answer to all questions as disturb; for doth not the Father take care of all? Then why worry? Why be afraid? For "He that is on the Lord's side, who may be against them?"

2502-1

WHEN EDGAR Cayce began suggesting to those who sought his help to study their own dreams as a source of guidance and information, I began to record mine. I discovered that symbols frequently occurred in different settings. For example, I noticed that in a number of my dreams a young, disreputable character appeared again and again. He smoked, seemed to be drunk at times, and frequently smiled slyly or winked at me. Gradually, I became afraid of him. In one dream, I met this character at night, leaning against a lamp-post on a dimly lit street. As I came near him, he threw a cigarette away and unexpectedly tackled me around the knees. We both fell to the ground and rolled around in filthy water that was running through the curb.

Upon awakening, I wrote down the dream. A few weeks later when I had gone back to look at it, I realized what the dream was trying to say. The dream was actually a warning and seemed to accurately foretell the possibility of my entanglement with a series of personal temptations. I should point out that this character looked very much like an ill-kempt me, and I decided that he was a symbol for my own lower self. Repeat-edly, in my dreams, he seemed to get into a variety of difficulties. Fi-nally, I began to pray for him. After I had started to pray, I remember in one dream he complained bitterly that I was taking unfair advantage. Nevertheless, I continued to pray. Afterwards, the frequency of the ap-pearance of this character lessened in my dreams and even my chal-lenges in waking life became easier. Prayer can be used in many different ways. In fact, the Cayce readings affirm the importance of both prayer and meditation as being instrumental in the process of spiritual growth and transformation.

Meditation is different than prayer. Many years ago, about one month after I had begun daily, thirty-minute meditation periods, I had a strange and rather beautiful meditation experience. It was spring, and I was seated looking out a window on the third floor of an oceanfront home. After following the quieting procedures for meditation (which are discussed later in this chapter) a stillness came over me that was extremely intense. All at once an incredible humming started in my head. It made me think of the sound electricity might make as it rushes through electrical wires. Then came the most beautiful music I have ever heard. I have no words with which to describe those sounds. It was an incredible experience in consciousness. Through the years, I have been diligent for long periods of time about working with meditation daily and, perhaps as a byproduct, I have had a variety of very interest-ing experiences in consciousness. For me, these experiences have veri-fied the fact that we are much more than a physical body and that there is a spiritual part of us that we can awaken and attune to.

In a reading given to a prayer group studying Cayce's information on prayer and meditation, Edgar Cayce clarified the relationship between these two practices.

First, in considering such, it would be well to analyze that difference (that is not always understood) between meditation and prayer.

As it has been defined or given in an illustrated manner by the Great Teacher, prayer is the *making* of one's conscious self more in attune with the spiritual forces that may manifest in a material world, and is *ordinarily* given as a *cooperative* experience of *many* individuals when all are asked to come in one accord and one mind...

Here we have drawn for us a comparison in prayer: That which may be the pouring out of the personality of the individual, or a group who enter in for the purpose of either outward show to be seen of men; or that enter in even as in the closet of one's inner self and pours out self that the inner man may be filled with the Spirit of the Father in His merciful kindness to men.

Now draw the comparisons for meditation: Meditation, then, is prayer, but is prayer from *within* the *inner* self, and partakes not only of the physical inner man but the soul that is aroused by the spirit of man from within . . .

Prayer is the concerted effort of the physical consciousness to become attuned to the consciousness of the Creator, either collectively or individually! *Meditation* is *emptying* self of all that hinders the creative forces from rising along the natural channels of the physical man to be disseminated through those centers and sources that create the activities of the physical, the mental, the spiritual man; properly done must make one *stronger* mentally, physically . . .   281-13

On another occasion, Edgar Cayce asked the prayer group to consider the following:

What *is* meditation?

It is not musing, not daydreaming; but as ye find your bodies made up of the physical, mental and spiritual, it is the attuning of the mental body and the physical body to its spiritual source.

281-41

Because of the importance the Edgar Cayce readings attribute to prayer and meditation, let us examine these two disciplines in greater detail.

The Importance of Working with Daily Prayer

At some point in almost every individual's life, he or she decides to deal with prayer in one way or another. For example, for many people in our Western culture, prayer is often regarded as a childhood experience suggested by parents or our religious upbringing. Oftentimes, it becomes something pushed aside as the routine and focus of daily life becomes more demanding. With prayer, as with meditation, it is important for us not only to know something about the nature of the subject but also to practice what is known with some diligence if results of a positive nature are to occur. Too often we may simply wait until we are facing an emergency, then quickly try to pray and expect magical results. Just like any other activity, the discipline of prayer should be something that is practiced regularly if an individual hopes to achieve personal aptitude. It is just like another other skill.

If you are just beginning to work with prayer, simply set aside ten or fifteen minutes each day for prayer and meditation. I would recommend beginning with prayer, then meditate, and then pray again. Later, you may wish to divide the time between prayer and meditation, as you begin to enjoy both disciplines and see the results in your life and how those results have affected others. However, remember to pray at least briefly for yourself and others after every meditation. You will see the advantages of this later.

It is important to deal concretely with situations and people as you pray. Work directly with God or with whatever you call the creative power of the universe. This may be done verbally aloud or in silence, using words or pictures. On one occasion, I remember meditating to the affirmation, "How gracious is Thy presence in the earth, O Lord." All at once, in my mind's eye I saw a beautiful white dogwood tree in full bloom, followed quickly by the image of my wife's smile. Obviously, each image was symbolic of my understanding of God's presence in the earth. In your own prayer practice, it's probably a good idea to experiment with various kinds of prayer—for example, prayers of praise and adoration, or prayers of thanksgiving, prayers of petition, or even prayers of confession.

Praise and adoration prayers can offer endless experiences of joy as we recognize the beauty and complexity of God's universe. The movement of an ant upon the sand, the loving gaze of a personal pet, the regular flow of ocean waves, the beauty of a sunrise, or the magnificence of a star-filled sky at night, can all provide innumerable opportunities for recognizing this Creative Force in expression all about us. Only as we begin to comprehend the presence of life everywhere are we able to fully sense our own part in the plan of Creation. Once we extend this type of prayer, every moment of the day can bring reasons for thoughts and words that express our new acceptance of God's grace and love.

Prayers of thanksgiving are also very helpful in our lives. Few of us say, "Thank you" often enough to our family and friends, much less to our Creator. In Scripture, the Psalms are literally filled with prayers of thanksgiving. There is a reason for that. These prayers can help us to become more aware of the many blessings we each possess in daily life. In order to escape meaningless repetition, we may wish to create our own prayers of thanksgiving. For example, saying grace before mealtimes can provide a continuous opportunity for the growth of our prayers and their change of expression.

Perhaps the most familiar types of prayers are prayers of petition. These prayers can be thought of as the expression of requests, hopes, desires, and the verbalization of an individual's needs, wants and wishes. With prayers of petition, it's important to end with, "God's will be done," since the Creator alone is aware of the highest good. Because we can become instruments of God's expression in the earth, even constructive thought can become a prayer. With prayers of petition, we can give a simple blessing, a hope expressed for protection, or even the simple thought of sending "light" to surround a name or a face. We can also offer a more sustained and focused petition for healing prayer.

In the case of working with focused, healing prayers, it's important to have obtained permission or a request from the person or family involved. Also, we need to be careful to seek God's will, not our own. Prayer groups can be especially helpful in studying and working with healing prayer. In fact, the prayer group begun by Edgar Cayce in 1931 is still active today through the work of A.R.E., offering prayers each month to literally thousands of individuals worldwide.

In petitionary prayer, it's important not to overlook our selves. In my own experience, meditation has frequently been almost impossible without prayer, and prayer has been greatly helped by meditation. Prayer for oneself is a way of recognizing the creative side of one's nature. It is also a way of expressing love of self, without which there can be little real love of others. Almost every individual has sought the help of a higher power in trying to meet difficult circumstances or personal trials, but how often have we remembered to seek attunement through prayer for our own illness and pain?

In one reading given to a twenty-four-year-old model and showgirl who was interested in overcoming various fears, Cayce emphasized the importance of personal prayer:

> When fear of the future occurs, or fear of the past, or fear of what others will say—put all such away with this prayer—not merely by mouth, not merely by thought, but in body, in mind and in soul say:
>
> *"Here am I, Lord—Thine! Keep me in the way Thou would have me go, rather than in that I might choose."*   2540-1

Every moment of silence is an opportunity for prayer. Sometimes, after a requested moment of silence before a lecture, I have emphasized this point my telling audiences that if I knew how individuals had spent that moment of silence, I could tell them where they were on their own spiritual path. It is important to become aware and cognizant of what we do with our opportunities for silence.

A final and very important kind of prayer is a prayer of confession.

Both the Catholic Church and psychiatry have developed the act of confession as a healing device. In my opinion, an individual can use it very effectively in clearing specific blocks, especially those of fear. For example, let us assume that you are afraid just prior to making a public speech. Try facing such a situation in a period of confessional prayer, in the quiet of your own heart and mind. See yourself talking before an audience: Admit the fear and feel it. Sense the tension in your own body. Speak to yourself, relax, turn loose, and let go. Feel the tension flow away. Reassure yourself that you can and will be able to handle such a situation. Don't do this just once. Try it again and again until you are ready to tackle the actual experience of speaking before a group. Pray that you can and will be able to handle the situation. By seriously working with this approach, you will gradually lose your fear to the point of being able to give the talk.

Many of us remain unaware of the blocks we store in our unconscious mind that involve fear of people. In order to address these blocks, you may wish to try the following exercise once each day for five days. Examine the results. You may be surprised at your changed attitude, which frequently will include a freedom from fear in relation to the person you have in mind:

Exercise: The Action of Grace in Your Life
In your mind, examine a *good* relationship by considering the following questions. For the exercise, sit relaxed, with your eyes closed, and visualize the person you have loved or do love the most. Read each question slowly before closing your eyes, and allow a whole minute to contemplate the answer before moving on to the next question.

1. Have you ever felt it desirable or necessary to protect this person physically? How?
2. Have you ever felt differently about this relationship than you feel now?
3. Do other people remind you of this person? How do you feel when you are reminded of this individual?
4. Do you have an economic relationship with this person?
5. How has this person/relationship helped you?
6. If you could imagine having had a past–life relationship with this

individual what might that relationship have been like?

7. Would you like to see this person in another life? In another relationship dynamic?

    a. Spend thirty seconds thinking about relating to this individual constructively.

    b. Pray for this individual in your own way for thirty seconds.

    c. In your own way, send love to this person for thirty seconds.

Using the same type of exercise, now it's time to examine one of the most difficult relationships you've experienced in life with another person, living or dead, For the exercise, sit relaxed, with your eyes closed, and visualize the face of that person. As you read and contemplate each of the following questions, try to see this person's face and hear her or his voice. As you did for the positive relationship, read each question slowly before closing your eyes, and allow a minute to contemplate the answer before moving on to the next question.

1. What is the most irritating thing that this person does?

2. Did you first love this person or did you have a different kind of relationship with this individual before having had difficulty with him or her?

3. Try to remember the first difficulty you had with this person—what was the basic cause of the problem?

4. Have you ever wanted to hit, hurt, or even kill this person?

5. Have you ever feared this person?

6. Are there physical characteristics about this person that you dislike very much?

7. Have you ever felt any other relationship dynamic with this person than the one that exists now (for example, feeling like the person acts like a father, a mother, a child, a sibling, a spouse, or a friend)?

    a. Spend thirty seconds forgiving yourself for specific things you did in the relationship.

    b. Silently in your own way, spend thirty seconds asking God forgiveness for your attitude in the past and/or the present.

    c. Silently, for thirty seconds, forgive the person for any hurt rendered you.

    d. In your own way, spend thirty seconds praying for this person—blessing her or him in the process.

In my own experience, I have found that as we extend and enrich our prayer life, nothing but good can come as a result.

The Importance of Working with Daily Meditation

Although working with the practice of meditation may not yet be as common in Western culture as the practice of prayer, the Edgar Cayce readings suggest that meditation is something that all individuals need to learn. Meditation can be instrumental in personal growth and development, as well as to further strengthen relationships that individuals have with themselves, with others, and with their God.

Most of us have never stopped to consider how much time and energy we spend on thinking about feeling various energized emotions that are stored as thought patterns related to the body's activities. By briefly reviewing the day's thoughts on such things as exercise, eating, and sex, we can see how much time and energy becomes focused on our body and our mind. It is the practice of meditation that can help to awaken the spiritual part of us that is often overlooked. Meditation can entail the quickening of the soul and the discovery of the eternal soul self. In fact, meditation is a practice that can bring together all components of the individual—body, mind, and spirit. The Edgar Cayce readings put it like this:

> As has been given, there are *definite* conditions that arise from within the inner man when an individual enters into true or deep meditation. A physical condition happens, a physical activity takes place! Acting through what? Through that man has chosen to call the imaginative or the impulsive, and the sources of impulse are aroused by the shutting out of thought pertaining to activities or attributes of the carnal forces of man.   281-13

In today's society many individuals have expressed their own spiritual awakening through an experience they describe of having been "born again." These individuals often describe their lives as having been transformed through the act of giving themselves to Christ or God. This can certainly be a very positive experience for individuals as long as the experience produces positive results and even life–changing approaches to dealing with and working with others in daily life.

A personal awakening that also includes meditation develops control of the mind and emotions, enabling the individual to sustain, enrich, and deepen the attunement. This can lead to the growth of new capacities for love for and service to others. The mystical literature of every major world religion testifies to this point of view. God literally speaks to us where we are, in our own temple and body–consciousness. As Paul, the New Testament writer of church letters who himself had a conversion experience wrote, " . . . ye are the temple of the living God." (2 Corinthians 6:16)

Thus, whether you are a "born–again" Christian, a religious intellectual, a proponent of ecumenical spirituality or New Age beliefs, or even a hardened materialist refusing to believe in things of a spiritual nature, if you try to work with the approaches of prayer and meditation you will find them helpful. At the same time, these practices will open you up to a broadened view of life and your potential contribution to the world at large.

The Cayce information presents a helpful perspective on the reason behind working with meditation. To be sure, that reason is not to experience altered states of consciousness or to instead learn how to relax (although both of these may be byproducts of meditation), instead the reason is essentially to allow the true nature of the soul self to manifest in the physical world:

> **For the Lord in His temple in thee meets thee there. Meditate upon those activities that may be motivative by the desires of the *inner* self, rather than the glorification of the material self.**
>
> **1189-1**

> **You have the meditation because you desire to be attuned with Creative Forces. You don't have the meditation because it's a duty or because you want to feel better, but to attune self to the infinite!**
>
> **1861-18**

It is important to point out that the Edgar Cayce readings are ecumenical in nature. They present a look at the universality of the Christ
Consciousness, which is described as the "awareness within each soul,
imprinted in pattern on the mind and waiting to be awakened by the
will of the soul's oneness with God." (5749–14) The readings also present
a universal look at the life of Jesus, suggesting that the example of his
life is not just appropriate for Christians but also for individuals from
every religious background. In fact, the readings suggest that Jesus ex-
emplified the attainment of the Christ Consciousness in a way that is
universally applicable:

> *All* must pass under the rod as of that *cleansing* necessary for the
> inflowing of the Christ Consciousness, even as *He* passed under
> the rod, partook of the cup—and *gives* same to others. See?
>
> 281-5

> Not so much self-development, but rather developing the Christ
> Consciousness in self, being selfless, that He may have *His* way
> with thee, that He—the Christ—may direct thy ways, that He will
> guide thee in the things thou doest, thou sayest.   281-20

> What *will* ye do with this man thy elder brother, thy Christ, who—
> that thy Destiny might be sure in Him—has shown thee the more
> excellent way. Not in mighty deeds of valor, not in the exaltation
> of thy knowledge or thy power; but in the gentleness of the things
> of the spirit: Love, kindness, longsuffering, patience; these thy
> brother hath shown thee that thou, applying them in thy
> associations with thy fellow man day by day, here a little, there
> a little, may become one with Him as He has *destined* that thou
> shouldst be!   849-11

As we awaken within ourselves these greater capacities for love and
service, we become more creative, and more attuned to our Creator.
This goal of meditation is indeed for the purpose of our own personal,
spiritual growth and development.

Much of the great mystical literature of every world religion contains deep descriptions of light-filled experiences during the process of personal attunement. In the same way, the Edgar Cayce readings on meditation make many references to light. For example, in one reading, a "light experience" is described in this fashion: "Thus, as we find, we will come to see not only the light but—by the deep meditation—may enter in and become a portion *of* the light that may bring helpful *healing* attributes *to* the psychological conditions in the body." (774-3)

Similarly, if we turn to the New Testament and Jesus' statements about light, we can now understand what these references to light may be suggesting: "Ye are the light of the world . . . Let your light so shine before men, that they may see your good works, and glorify your Father which is in heaven." (Matthew 5:14, 16) "I am the light of the world . . ." (John 8:12) "The light of the body is the eye: if therefore thine eye be single, thy whole body shall be full of light." (Matthew 6:22) This last verse may especially be a direct reference to meditation and the attunement of the third eye—a major chakra of the body called the pituitary, which will be discussed later. With this in mind, discovering the light becomes symbolically or perhaps even literally a goal of meditation.

Interestingly, the readings describe meditation as a way of preparing for the afterlife; consider this statement:

> These become hard at times for the individual to visualize; that the mental and soul may manifest without a physical vehicle. Yet in the deeper meditations, in those experiences when those influences may arise when the spirit of the Creative Force, the universality of soul, of mind—not as material, not as judgments, not *in* time and space but *of* time and space—may become lost in the Whole, instead of the entity being lost in the maze of confusing influences—then the soul visions arise in the meditations. 987-4

Most of us spend a great deal of time and energy wrestling with ourselves, fighting the thought forms that we continue to feed and build each time we allow our mind and emotions to dwell on negative thought processes. Self-pity, anger, hate, and lust are well known emotions, but one of the most destructive is fear. It has many faces. Working with meditation and channeling some of our creative energies inwardly through the higher centers rather than directing it outwardly as we do in anger, sex, self-pity, and so on, is recommended as an integral part of our plan to redirect the energies we use in fear experiences.

What exactly happens when we meditate, opening ourselves to a spiritual purpose, a spiritual alignment of the body and mind? As I understand it, there is a direct movement of the energy from the Leydig (gonad–adrenal) area of the body to the pineal center (near the top of the crown) and then to the control center, the pituitary or third eye. Imagining that this can be symbolized by a cup, the well-known phrase from the Twenty-third Psalm takes on new meaning with the expression, "My cup runneth over." Edgar Cayce describes the connection of these spiritual centers, as follows:

> In the body we find that which connects the pineal, the pituitary, the lyden, may be truly called the silver cord, or the golden cup that may be filled with a closer walk with that which is the creative essence in physical, mental and spiritual life . . . 262-20

Much of the world is in fragmentation and chaos because of imbalance. In large measure, the West has attempted to master the outer, physical world but has long neglected the inner, spiritual world. Conversely, there are places in the East where the outer world has been deemed unimportant and adepts have attempted to obtain mastery over the inner self. A balance between these two expressions is suggested in the Edgar Cayce readings. Rather than attempting to escape or ignore the physical world, the readings suggest that part of our task is to somehow manifest *spirit* into physical activity. With this in mind, part of our goal for being in physical consciousness should be to bring spirit into the earth. Prayer and meditation can be invaluable tools for achieving this new consciousness, as well as a release from our fears, especially those related to fear of God, neighbor, and self.

How to Begin Meditation

It's actually not that difficult to make meditation and prayer an active part of your daily life. To begin, choose a period of fifteen minutes that you can set aside each day specifically for this purpose. Using the same time and same place can be very helpful for individuals wanting to establish the habit.

As you begin, you may wish to play some soothing music in the background as you are adjusting your body. Your spine should be straight, as if there were an imaginary line from the center of your head to the base of your spine. It can be helpful to relax the head and neck muscles by moving your head, slowly, forward, backward, and to each side three or four times. Always begin from an upright position and then rotate your head first one way and then in the opposite direction. This movement increases circulation through the upper gland centers.

Next, you may wish to work with some breathing exercises. One suggestion is to take three deep breaths, breathing slowly through the right nostril and then exhaling slowly through the mouth. Afterward, take three deep breaths slowly through the left nostril and then exhale through the right. This exercise can also stimulate the circulation and help an individual come to full consciousness.

After these exercises, you may wish to read, silently or aloud, some inspirational passage from scripture. If you don't have your own selection, Edgar Cayce often recommended biblical passages, such as John 14, 15, 16 and 17, or an inspiring psalm. Others may choose to read passages from material such as the Bhagavad-Gita, the Persian poets, or any other inspirational verse.

For some, incense can be helpful during this preparatory period, as well as the meditation itself. Others may choose to chant—Cayce recommended simple chants such as the syllable, "ohm," repeated slowly five to seven times, or chanting simple vowel sounds, "a . . . e . . . i . . . o . . . u . . . " Working with meditation in a small group can also be very helpful, as well as meditating with a friend or even meditating at the same time as others, even when they are not physically present.

After these preparatory exercises, the next step is to focus the mind on a proper affirmation. "What is a proper affirmation?" you may ask.

Edgar Cayce suggested that since mind is the builder, it is important to focus a meditating mind upon a positive affirmation that will enable the individual to become a better person as well as to more fully attune to those spiritual qualities already residing deep within the soul. You may wish to meditate on a simple affirmation, such as "I am at Peace," or "God is Love," or you might want to consider a few of the affirmations recommended for meditation by Edgar Cayce:

> Not my will but Thine, O Lord, be done in and through me. Let me ever be a channel of blessings, today, now, to those that I contact, in every way. Let my going in, mine coming out be in accord with that Thou would have me do, and as the call comes, "Here am I, send me, use me!"   262-3

> Father, as we seek to see and know Thy face, may we each, as individuals, and as a group, come to know ourselves, even as we are known, that we—as lights in Thee—may give the better concept of Thy Spirit in this world.   262-5

> Create in me a pure heart, O God! Open Thou mine heart to the faith Thou hast implanted in all that seek Thy face! Help thou mine unbelief in my God, in my neighbor, in myself!   262-13

> As my body, mind and soul are one, Thou, O Lord, in the manifestations in the earth, in power, in might, in glory, art One. May I see in that I do, day by day, more of that realization, and manifest the more.   262-38

> Open thou mine eyes, O God, that I may know the glory Thou hast prepared for me.   262-89

> Let the knowledge of the Lord so permeate my being that there is less and less of self, more and more of God, in my dealings with my fellow man; that the Christ may be in all, through all, in His Name.   262-95

Affirmations such as these contain statements of spiritual purposes and goals. They focus attention on new commitments of love and service. They are more than this, however. As you continue to hold one of these affirmations, first as words, then in terms of total meaning, and finally as an inner quickening or movement, you will awaken the spiritual purposes buried deep within your real or soul self.

As an experiment, try taking one of these affirmations apart word for word. Consider the meaning of each word for you. It may help you to write this out or discuss and share your observations with other people who are also working with these same affirmations. In fact, some of these affirmations have references to the group meditation process. The affirmation is the key to inner movement. It may work as follows:

The mind seems to be present in the very cell structure of the body tissue. Each moment, literally millions of cells are dying and millions of others are being reborn. It is possible that thought energy impregnated with spiritual patterns gradually attunes more and more of the physical vibrations of the body to the soul's model and pattern. In this way there is both an awakening stimulus and an alignment process. All it takes to meditate effectively is determination.

Persistence in meditation brings quietness. For many individuals, with quietness comes light. However, these are only signs along the way. Inner changes come so quickly, sometimes so unobtrusively, that others may notice a difference even before the meditator does—your anger may no longer be instantaneous; you may feel greater joy in little experiences; a personal fear may have disappeared.

Results of Meditation

What can we expect as results of meditation? Perhaps at this point a brief description of the first physical and mental reactions to meditation will be helpful. The body demands attention: the chair may be hard or the mouth dry; tension and itching may be experienced; and so on. Physical sensations differ according to the condition of the person. At the same time, the conscious mind may jump quickly from one thought to another in an endless sequence. Suddenly, consciousness may be flooded by a series of strange pictures, colors, faces, or scenes. They come from the unconsciousness and should simply be ignored and set aside or else they can take away from the true purpose of meditation. As individuals persist in daily meditation practice sessions, a quietness of the body and mind will result.

Many people notice greater body control as the first good effects of meditation. It is possible to quiet the mind more quickly. Short periods of rest and sleep come easily and renew body energies. For a short time, a person may become more aware of bodily discomforts, but then there are readjustments, bringing healing. As one reading puts it:

> **Thus a meditation, a centralizing, a localizing of the mind upon those portions of the system affected, or upon the activities needed for the physical being, *influences*, directs the principal forces of the system, And it does resuscitate.   1992-3**

Gradually, the conscious mind becomes more controllable. It becomes possible to give up negative thoughts of gossip, filth, violence, fear, and so on. It is important to recognize that meditation does not result in some special vision or experience that overwhelms the meditator, but rather in a gradual change of one's whole life pattern, a refocusing on a more positive or spiritual attitude.

Long-range results of meditation may include greater activity of the three higher endocrine gland centers (chakras)—the thyroid (throat area), the pineal (crown), and the pituitary (third eye). The thyroid seems to be related to will power, which increases. Most of us know what we should be doing, we simply do not have the will to do it. Meditation strengthens the will. The pineal center involves memory, knowledge of the soul itself. Its awakening or opening may offer knowledge of what one needs to move ahead, to grow. A new talent may develop, or recognition of the right direction for action, or identification of an old friend from another time and place. Finally, the pituitary can bring new capacities for service. One becomes a better channel for healing and a more creative and loving person.

Meditation is a lighted path. As an individual begins to work with regular meditation, the shadows of fear can be dispelled. At the same time, as fear is alleviated from an individual's consciousness, he or she can begin to more fully live a purposeful and creative life.

Experiences and Warnings

Experiences during meditation are almost as varied as the individuals who meditate. Some of the more frequently reported experiences include tingling along the spine and limbs; fullness and tightness in various gland centers; heat, especially in the hands and head; awareness of body noises not usually heard; seeming movement of the body back and forth, from side to side, or a spinning sensation; coolness on the forehead; seeming elongation, or swelling of the body; sense of being out of body; and pain in the head or in other parts of the body. For the most part, these are very normal realignments, adjustments, and awareness of circulation flow and nerve energy. If such sensations are overwhelming, stop and pray; then go on.

There are warnings, however, that should be kept in mind for any student interested in meditation. In general, these warnings can be classified under three headings: physical difficulties, ego trips in a world of illusion, and fear of the unknown. In a number of different readings, Edgar Cayce warned people who were suffering from bodily malfunctions to stop meditating until the body was in better physical condition. Sometimes such things as a bad spinal alignment, the use of heavy drugs or a glandular imbalance were described as being the cause of the problem. It was only after the cause had been addressed, cured, or healed that the readings would recommend the practice of further meditation.

In addition to these warnings, psychiatry has long known that our unconscious mind contains some very real "demons" of hate, fear, and so on. We often store memories of failures, hurts, and guilt. There are relationships and issues from our past that are loaded with fear, hurt, and anger. We also have attachments related to the love of money, power, or possessions. To avoid encountering these issues in meditation as the unconscious is awakened, it's important to set a spiritually focused ideal before meditating and to use a spiritually focused affirmation.

Finally, there are people who fear meditation as a door to the inner world. Such individuals need to address these fears, in the same way that all of our fears need to be addressed. Sometimes, doubting one's own value and a lack of self-love can be involved in this type of fear. As one persists in meditation, loneliness and doubt of God and self fade, because the real soul–self awakens and it becomes very clear that there is much more to us and our deep connection to God than we may have ever dared to imagine.

The Place of Small Groups and Service in Bringing Your Spiritual Life into Alignment

Perhaps one of the most important sets of materials Edgar Cayce provided for individuals interested in his work is the information he gave on spiritual growth, personal transformation, and the application of universal laws in everyday life. Beginning in 1931, this information took on a special emphasis in the activity of small groups of people who were encouraged to study the process of spiritual growth together. Even today, these ecumenical, spiritual growth discussion groups meet in individual homes around the world, studying concepts like meditation, cooperation, patience, fellowship, and love.

In addition to learning about meditation and universal principles, groups often discuss dreams and overcoming personal challenges; and they generally select a spiritual "experiment" or a discipline as a group, applying it in their daily life until the next meeting

How can such a group assist you in dealing with fear? There are three ways in which I have seen group action help people with fears, including myself. My experience with such work covers many decades. First, group action augments and sharpens our capacity to acquire self-knowledge; second, the group energy and support provides psychological and vibratory protection; and, third, a group of people working together can speed and amplify the healing process.

More information about where these groups are meeting near you, studying these universal laws and the volumes *A Search for God, Book I* and *Book II*, is available from A.R.E.

In regards to service, the readings were especially clear on the importance of individuals reaching out to others as a means of overcoming problems in their own lives. The following selections are just a few of the literally hundreds that were given on this topic:

(Q) How can I overcome fear of advancing old age and being alone?
(A) By going out and doing something for somebody else; that is, those not able to do for themselves, making others happy, forgetting self entirely. These are as material manifestations but in helping someone else you'll get rid of your feelings. 5226-1

When one understands self, and self's relation to its Maker, the duty to its neighbor, its own duty to self, it cannot, it will not be false to man, or to its Maker ... What one thinks continually, they become; what one cherishes in their heart and mind they make a part of the pulsation of their heart, through their own blood cells, and build in their own physical, that which its spirit and soul must feed upon . . .   3744-5

(Q) Has [my] husband anything to do with this condition of depression and general unhappiness?
(A) Arising from those fears that have arisen in the present from the activities during this particular period ... This is rather from within self, but losing self in aid for others—and in doing that which gives joy to the inner self will relieve much of these.
**   1928-1**

Let that which causes doubt or fear be taken up in the willingness, the desire, to be of help to others.   69-4

Perhaps the simple answer as to why service to others can be helpful in overcoming personal fears is because service is the act of reaching out to others. Since fear is so concerned with one's self, as we shift our attention onto the needs of others, this focus on self's issues and problems can begin to lessen. In fact, the negative energy that has paralyzed us can be transformed into joyous relationships with others. Just as importantly, as we begin to express our love for others, we are able to accept more readily God's love for us.

Symbols of the Self

Finally, as we conclude this section on meditation, let us consider dreams as the language of the unconscious, which can help us understand one of the ways we have kept the mystery of our own spiritual nature alive through the ages. I must admit right away that this is an inadequate treatment of a very complicated subject and that it is also a personal interpretation. However, it is my hope that these suggestions will start you searching for your own inner symbology. By so doing, you will begin to learn the language of your own unconscious and begin to deal more directly with new aspects of yourself.

I have often called dreams the "language" of the unconscious. Through our dreams we can come to understand a great source of symbols within ourselves. These symbols are personal, cultural, and universal (or archetypal). We build up personal and cultural symbols around thought forms constructed out of our experiences. Universal symbolism is our way of recognizing and using symbols preserved by groups and masses of people through ritual, art forms, legends, fairy tales, and so on. Many of these symbols come to us as a means of keeping alive an inner knowledge of the spiritual self.

According to the Edgar Cayce information, some of these universal symbols are stored deep within our physical bodies and can be awakened in meditation. This is especially relevant, for example, when discussing the chakras and their corresponding endocrine centers. Just briefly, those endocrine centers are:

- the gonads (groin area)
- the cells of Leydig (interstitial cells contained in the gonads and the adrenals)
- the adrenals (solar plexus area)
- the thymus (heart center)
- the thyroid (neck or will center)
- the pineal (top of head)
- the pituitary (third eye)

From Cayce's perspective, while we are in a flesh body the soul functions through these centers. In addition, as we begin to work with meditation, our thought forms related to the activity of these centers—in
other words, the ways in which we function at each of these levels—are
stimulated. We often become conscious of rediscovering these aspects
of ourselves around us and in our dreams. Some of these images can be
frightening, but oftentimes these fear-laden patterns are our own cre-
ations at the level of the mind. You may wish to consider beginning a
personal search of these gland symbols and discovering their meaning
for you.

For example, let's start with an experience from the Old Testament
that shows how these symbols can be brought to personal awareness.
In the book of Ezekiel, the prophet had an experience in which he saw
a whirlwind with the face of a bull, the face of an androgynous man, the
face of a lion, and the face of an eagle. Interestingly enough, these images are the universal symbols for the gonads (bull), the cells of Leydig
(androgynous man), the adrenals (lion) and the thymus (eagle). With
this in mind, what do these four figures represent to you?

One man wrote Edgar Cayce that he had often dreamed since childhood of a lion running after him, pulling him down and beginning to
eat his flesh. Cayce told him that his anger (symbolized by the lion) was
actually destroying body tissue within himself. Later, the man admitted
to overwhelming fits of uncontrolled rage.

Take a look at your own dreams. When you're at home, examine the
pictures you have decided to put on your walls. Take a look at the
knick-knacks on your mantel and even the designs on your clothing or
jewelry. What do you have placed on your desk or file cabinet at work?
You may find some of these figures. Do you like the image of the power
associated with having a tiger in your tank? Would you insist on taking
time to see a bull fight while in Mexico or Spain? Do you enjoy watching male impersonators or women, perhaps outwardly demonstrating
issues related to the balance of male-female energies? Does the eagle
symbolize for you freedom and the ability to soar to great heights or
does it suggest incredible power and mastery over the skies.

Even in fairy tales universal symbolism can touch upon issues related to our daily lives and personal experiences while in the earth. For

example, what if Snow White is a symbol of spirit coming into the earth and finding herself living with seven little men (seven spiritual chakras)? What if Dopey is one way we can express our sexual energy while in the earth—remember, he lined up twice to be kissed by Snow White and he was able to out dance all the others. Perhaps Grumpy symbolizes one possible outlet of the activity of the adrenals.

It might be that the seven churches of the Revelation actually relate to these seven centers. In fact, Edgar Cayce suggests that this book of the Bible is actually an advanced symbolic study of what occurs within the individual during meditation.

These universal symbols are all around us. The following list shows some possible symbols for the seven glandular centers collected from metaphysical literature, the Bible, legends, fairy tales, and so on. Symbols like these might cause us to ponder what kinds of deeper universal meanings are connected with their imagery:

• The seven churches of the New Testament
• The seven knots on the rope Mohammed saw hanging from heaven
• The seven steps on Mayan pyramids
• The seven sisters of the Pleiades
• The seven dwarfs who lived with Snow White

If indeed we can sense that there are seven major centers of light within ourselves, the points at which the soul functions through the flesh body, then perhaps through prayer and meditation the higher centers can be awakened and the energies can flow downward to heal and transform the energies within the lower centers. It is here that fear patterns can be locked in place and it is the processes of meditation and prayer that can transform these patterns into more constructive avenues of expression. The importance of these practices cannot be overstated in the process of an individual's own spiritual growth and transformation. With this in mind, the Cayce readings told one individual: "Don't let a day go by without meditation and prayer for some definite purpose, and not for self, but that self may be the channel of help to someone else. For in helping others is the greater way to help self." (3624–1)

8

Bringing Your Life into Alignment– Mentally

And keep an even mental balance. Don't worry! It is easy to say "Don't worry," but how may a person prevent it? By keeping control of the mind, not only through the very will of self but by keeping occupied in doing something for others.   646-1

WE COME now to what may well be the most important step for overcoming patterns of fear and anxiety—using the mind as a constructive, helpful tool rather than as a tool for emphasizing the problem.

Most of us assume that we are rational human beings who do a certain amount of creative thinking. However, oftentimes what we call thinking is simply a set of responses to stimuli. All too often we are creatures of habit and don't necessarily become conscious of what we are thinking and doing. Can you recall the last two individuals you spoke with by telephone? What colors are most prominent on your screen when you open your e-mail? How difficult is it to remember what you had for dinner the night before last? Can you recall the last person who asked you, "How are you?" and what your response to that question was? In addition to our automatic responses to individuals and experiences, we have created strong habit patterns with our minds and many of these patterns reflect our fears—although we rarely think of them in this connection.

For example, have you ever said, "I'm afraid I'm going to be late?" Or, "I'm afraid I won't be able to do that?" Or, in reference to some segment of society, how often have you said, "I don't like _____," or "I don't understand _____." Do you often think, "I'll never be able to lose the weight" or "I'll never get that job?" How frequently do you reinforce a state of confusion with statements such as, "I don't know what I am going to do about it?" Frequently, behind many of these phrases can be found patterns of prejudice, self-pity, doubt, and other negative emotions, which are all breeding grounds for fear. The power of the mind in helping to overcome our previous response patterns and modes of behavior cannot be overestimated.

One of the most interesting experiences along these lines occurred while I was overseas during World War II. At the time, our company lived in cold, damp barracks in England. Things became even colder and damper when we were stationed in France. Unfortunately, because of these conditions, I developed a never-ending series of colds and sinus infections.

On returning home, back to the United States, I talked continuously about my sinus condition. The topic became a frequent focus of my thoughts and my words. Friends soon learned not to ask me how I felt, for I would tell them—in many oft-repeated words and phrases—about my condition. In fact, I frequently found myself saying things like, "I am afraid that I am going to have another attack of sinus." One morning, I awoke from a dream of being smothered. I had to get up and walk at five o'clock in the morning in the yard in order to catch my breath. I could feel the fear associated with having the sinus condition affect my routine.

It was then that I decided to give up my sinus problem, including the small polyps that had developed in my nose. I made a conscious decision to give up the attitude I had been holding regarding the problem. I let lose of the fear and worry and instead focused my mind on positive thoughts related to my health—thoughts like: "I am a healthy individual," "My breathing is deep, clear, refreshing, and bringing healing elements to my entire being," etc. By working with positive thoughts and ideas, I soon found that the difficulties I had been having with sinus began to disappear. In fact, in a very short time, the sinus condition and the polyps were gone altogether. Never again have I said, "I am afraid I am going to have a sinus attack."

The following extract from the Cayce readings is a good example of how often we subtly and repetitiously create fear patterns. Cayce gave the advice to a fifty-three-year-old woman:

> How, ye ask, is this applicable in the experience of this entity now known as or called [793]? That will, that fear of what may become a part of the experience is such in the experience of the entity that so oft does it find and has it found this very condition *preventing* self from enjoying even its greater joys. For so oft is the attitude, "Yes—but tomorrow is a change. Yes—but can that be true for me? Yes—but I have not accomplished that which is my ideal. Yes—but I have fallen short of that as I would do. Yes—but they will soon be grown, thinking their own thoughts, doing their own ways.
>
> And the entity has let so much of this *interfere* with and prevent the real joy of the beauties, the joys, the wonderful grace that has ever been and is so near to each soul that seeks to know His face.
>
> For it is not in some great deed, not in some great form. But just being kind, being gentle, being patient, being longsuffering, showing brotherly love, doing this or that for the sake of the very force that has prompted and does prompt self, is the manner in which each soul may *know* that "My Spirit, my soul, beareth witness with His Spirit that I am indeed His." And in this manner does one become aware of one's soul's presence with this house of clay.   793-2

Regardless of how accustomed we may have become to filling our minds with negative and destructive patterns of thinking, it is possible to completely refocus the activities of the mind into a much more helpful and constructive tool for effecting personal change. The following eight suggestions, including some detailed techniques, can help you build a fear-free, constructive life. Every step will strengthen and feed the thought forms that you build and thus will support your overall program of change. Each suggestion is explained in further detail. In all of these approaches, the focus is on becoming cognizant of where you are placing the focus of your mind in the present:

1. **Set and Work with Spiritual Ideals**
2. **Focus on Constructive Thoughts**
3. **Use the Mind to Influence the Body**
4. **Cultivate Systematic Control of Thought**
5. **Use Inspirational Reading**
6. **Watch Your Dreams as a Means of Observing Your Real Attitude**
7. **Use Presleep Suggestion**
8. **Develop Your Sense of Humor**

1. Set and Work with Spiritual Ideals

Many Edgar Cayce readings explain the importance of setting ideals—physically, mentally, and spiritually. On multiple occasions, they go so far as to suggest that this activity is perhaps the single most important thing that individuals can do as a means of changing their lives and transforming their old response patterns into more positive behaviors. In a reading given to a fifty-seven-year-old divorced writer, the information explained exactly how this could be accomplished:

Analyze self and the purposes, the motives, the influences; and know that they agree with that which is thy ideal.

What is thy ideal? spiritually, mentally, physically?

Not what you would wish God to do for you, but what may you do in appreciation of the love shown?

Not as to what ye would like to be, but what may ye mentally

give that will be conducive to constructive thinking in the
experience of others?

In the physical, not what you want others to do for you, but
what may you do for them?

These are what we mean by constructive thinking, and as they
are applied within the experience we will come to see what a
spiritual life means. Not the eliminating of pleasures, for the
purpose of life *is* pleasure, but that which is constructive and not
destructive!   1995-1

For a seventeen-year-old student, the advice was even more specific:

What are the ideals? In physical relationships, in mental relationships and in spiritual relationships?

Know that ye are in the earth as an opportunity for self, for
social unfoldment and in the relationships with thy companions
of both thine own sex and the opposite sex you should not be
merely an idealist, but so live, not necessarily what is called a
puritanic life but so live that others, all others would wish to be
like [5256]. That is an ideal manner of conduct.

What is required in this? In self knowing thine own ideals,
spiritually, mentally, materially, not merely as "I think this
should be it, I think that would be wonderful, that this or that"
but write them down on paper and see what they look like. You'll
be surprised how oft you can change them from one day to
another.

Then, knowing the ideal, practice it. Don't have an ideal and
then not practice it in thy daily activities.   5256-1

Another woman was encouraged to use ideals as a means of overcoming her worry and fear:

One that is at times easily worried at material things. One that
at times worries as respecting the application others make of
their abilities. In the matter of worry, this—in its last analyses—
is that of fear. Fear is an enemy to the mental development of an

entity, changing or wavering the abilities of an entity in many directions . . .

Find that, that is the answer ever for self, as to *an* ideal to be worked toward, to be used at all times, to be leaned upon in adversity and in criticism, in successes, in failures, in pleasures, in hardships, in adversity and in those conditions that are as entanglements of the mental or physical being.   2501-1

With all the above in mind, how might you put your ideals on paper so that you can gradually change and review them? The following format shows two possible methods. Each has advantages. Use the one that is easiest for you. Understanding that "mind is the builder," do not neglect this exercise if you are serious about working with your own fears.

Format A: The Columned Approach to Working with Ideals

Many individuals have found that the key to working with a spiritual ideal is to use one of the concepts frequently mentioned in Edgar Cayce's readings, "Spirit is the Life; Mind is the Builder; and the Physical is the Result." To begin, the first step entails taking a sheet of paper and drawing three columns. Label the first "My Spiritual Ideal," label the second "My Mental Attitudes," and label the third "My Physical Activities."

The Cayce material suggests that, ultimately, a spiritual ideal is the highest spiritual quality or attainment that you could hope to have motivating you in your life right now. Although you are encouraged to choose a challenging spiritual ideal, it's recommended that the spiritual ideal chosen be something you can understand, work with, and see progressively manifested in your life. For some, this might be the pattern set by a spiritual example, such as Jesus, Buddha, Abraham, or Mohammed, for others it might be a quality such as love. In order to begin working with ideals, however, you should choose a quality or an attribute that really needs to be cultivated in your own life. For example, perhaps you may decide that you need to be more "patient" or more "forgiving" or more "understanding" in your interactions with others. Ideals grow and change as you do, so it's important to pick something with which you can really begin to work. For this exercise, let's say that your spiritual ideal is currently going to be *compassion*, so "compassion" would be written under the first column labeled "My Spiritual Ideal."

Under the second column, you need to begin listing "My Mental Attitudes." This column will contain those attitudes that will help build that spirit of compassion into your activities and your relationships with others and with your self. Perhaps you'll decide that "understanding" is an attitude you would like to cultivate in a frustrating relationship with a parent. Maybe "openness" is the mental attitude you want to begin holding in regard to one of your children with whom you've been having difficulty; and possibly "patience" best describes that attitude you need to use with your self.

The third column is the most detailed. It's the one place you can write out all those physical activities that you can begin doing in order to cultivate the mental attitude that reflects your spiritual ideal. For example, in the case of a frustrating parent with whom you are attempting to cultivate "understanding," perhaps each of the following would be appropriate activities to help build that same attitude: "practice attentive listening, rather then thinking what I am next going to say." "Make a list of the interests we share in common." "Begin praying that I will have the determination to keep on keeping on," etc. Each of your mental attitudes should have corresponding activities that will enable you to bring your spiritual ideal into the material world.

My Spiritual Ideal	My Mental Attitudes	My Physical Activities
Compassion	1. Understanding 2. Openness 3. Patience 4. Etc.	In Regards to <u>Understanding</u>: • Practice attentive listening • Make a list of the interests we share in common • Begin praying that I will have the determination to keep on keeping on In Regards to <u>Openness</u>:

Format B: The Bull's Eye Approach to Working with Ideals

This format accomplishes the same thing but is more detailed in terms of focusing your ideals chart on people and events that are a part of your daily activities. You will fill in the chart for each quadrant, in terms of those attitudes and activities that are especially relevant for the quadrant you are working on. For example, let's imagine that you are using the examples cited above and focusing your chart on your relationship with a parent, with your children, with your job, and with your self. Each portion of the quadrant would be filled in but the portion of the chart describing your relationship with a parent, for example, might begin to be filled out as follows:

The readings emphasize the fact that ideals will change and grow as you begin to change yourself. What is perhaps most practical about working with spiritual ideals is that they enable individuals to change automatic response patterns of negative behaviors and modes of expression into more constructive channels.

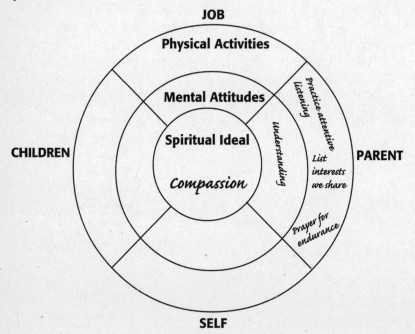

2. Focus on Constructive Thoughts

Constructive attitudes are essentially built of thoughts that are reactions to events in which you have been involved or to what you have heard, seen, or read about a particular condition, person, situation, or group. We all constantly add to or modify our attitudes. Every time we think, speak, or act while holding a particular attitude, we strengthen or change it slightly. Consider personal attitudes regarding fear. Every time we react negatively, we add to our negative thought patterns and we give greater power to that fear. Conversely, every time we react in a more positive manner, we lessen the strength of the fear pattern as we face it.

Review your habit patterns of speech. How often, when you are asked to do something or take part in an activity, do you say something like, "I am afraid I can't do that"? The truth of the matter is that there are a variety of ways to answer questions that are much better than "I am afraid." Instead, you might say, "It's not going to be possible," or even "No." If you are uncertain as to the answer, a possible response might be something like, "I'll try." We must stop telling ourselves in a variety of ways that we are afraid. Reflecting upon your own personal experiences might make the reason for this even clearer.

The following Edgar Cayce readings also emphasize the importance of constructive attitudes. Each was given for a person seeking help:

> **(Q) What causes the entity to complain of ailments so often and are they real or imaginative?**
> **(A) As is seen from that given, imaginative forces are manifested ever in the entity—but *fear* entering in, brings for a physical being that which becomes as real as were they disordered. Hence the ideal in body, in mind, in attainment, must be ever kept before the entity, and that the whole well-rounded life is *necessary* for the complete success in any phase of one's experience.**   **2686-1**

> **But do not become impatient with self nor the lack of those materializations at once of those hopes in the body. For ye grow in grace, in knowledge and in understanding. Where it has taken**

years to produce a fear, a doubt, an activity that begins to find
manifestation in the twitching of a muscle, in the expansion of
a vein, in the frustrations in the body forces—be patient, be quiet
within; and we will find those administrations that have been
made—and that may be made—will aid thee in growing in the
right directions.   3051-3

Also know that hate, jealousy, animosity, fear and the like, create
that environ, that animation, which—as it comes into material
manifestation—brings doubt, heartaches, tears, disappointments.
Oft one may question self as to why, or as to how such and such
could have come upon self, with all the high-minded ideas that
may be expressed. As has been indicated, that which we are
indeed speaks so loud, seldom is there heard what we say—other
than of a creative and constructive nature.   2131-1

As we find, first there must be, if there would be helpful forces
for this body, the changes of the mental attitude toward self,
toward general surroundings. There must be the holding to
some general creative energies, for the body will gain much
more by trying and in helping someone else, rather than pitying
or excusing or condemning things in [self or] others.   5123-1

This matter of building constructive attitudes each day in your personal thought processes becomes very practical in the following extract:

(Q) Will my business continue to be a success?
(A) As known or viewed from the very activities of self, if there
are to be continued the torments within self, the indecisions
within self, the expectancy that disorders or disruptions will
arise, these create those very influences in the contacts, in the
groups, in the relations that are necessary in the activities. But,
if there is shown faith, hope, understanding, cooperation in the
activities, it will continue not only to be as the present—but an
increased success; for there is the spirit of valuation and

> protection, for those very ideals that self would build within self.
>
> 290-1

Repeatedly, the readings advised individuals that they needed to change their mental attitude if they truly desired to overcome their fears and anxieties. In a very real sense, fear breeds more fear, making any anxieties or worries even worse in the process. However, constructive patterns of thought can be instrumental in transforming a fear into a more constructive response pattern. In addition to overcoming the fear, constructive thoughts can also transform an individual's perception of self, of self's fears and anxieties, and of self's ability to overcome any problem.

3. Use the Mind to Influence the Body

The power of the mind to influence physical body functions results in what has come to be known as psychosomatic effects. For example, a hypochondriac who merely *thinks* he or she is sick may actually become ill. Bodily tissues can become altered by emotion-laden thought. Long before the term psychosomatic had even been coined, Edgar Cayce noted the disruption of function and the destruction of bodily tissue because of an individual's thought processes. Perhaps of even greater importance is his position on the healing power of the mind when motivated by spiritual ideals and attitudes:

> As to the abilities of the entity in the present, then, and that to which it may attain, and how:
>
> Keep and make a balance in self, as indicated. Not only for that pertaining to the physical and mental, but that purposefulness for which the activities may be; and knowing for what expression there is that purposefulness in thine own spiritual self.
>
> For Mind is the Builder; but unless it be founded in that influence not made by might and power, but by the spirit of truth, of justice, of hope, of patience, of understanding, it may become a stumblingblock to the individual.
>
> And as the activities of self are to be in those fields in which

there is to be the influence upon the lives and the experiences
of many, all the more reason why these shall be founded in the
spirit of hope, of justice, of mercy, of patience, of love. 1094-1

In the spiritual life, keep close to that as has been accorded in the
mental forces of the body—knowing that in the understanding of
the relationships of the spiritual body there must be need of the
mental and physical for its material manifestation; though,
that—whatever there may be conceived by the mind of a body,
it finds *its* replica in a material experience; for with the body,
mind and spirit does one present itself *wholly* acceptable *unto*
the divine, *whatever* that may be made in the terms of worship-
fulness; for *in* the spiritual one lives, moves, and has one's
being—and the spirit is willing, and the flesh will follow, will the
mental [if the mental will] build in that direction that they are
kept in accord one with another.   454-1

Another reading, given for a thirty–six–year–old sales manager, clearly
states the potentially negative effects of the mind and the imaginative
forces without the presence of constructive thought. It also provides
some recommendations for personal balance, as well as suggestions for
keeping the mind more positive:

In the physical—here, as has been given, the body should be most
mindful, that the body is kept physically fit. Warnings have been
given the body. It isn't that there may be those additions or
reductions that may bring the body to a normal reaction, but
rather that the body-physical and body-mental may be kept in
or near normalcy, that the conditions as arise from day to day
may be met as is needed.

Then, play as well as work. Relax as well as keep taut. So,
through the mental abilities of the body, be as appreciative of
the finer things of life as of material success. Be as capable of
appreciating the beggar with a God-given voice as would bring
tears of appreciation of love of man for man or woman, or of the
appreciation of the beauties in nature, as appreciative of the man

with a million, able to wield a power and influence of a nature that shows and belies of self-aggrandizement of power. Be, through the mental abilities, so as to be appreciative of that in art, or beauty in a picture, or beauty in nature. Let these, as they did to thine own peoples—even thine prophet, thine servant David, as he declared in, "The glory of God is made manifest!— Even the heavens declare His glory, and the firmament showeth His handiwork"; for fame and fortune often take wings and fly away—but one appreciative of the beauties in nature, in the abilities of His handmaid in the might of Him that serves in song or dance, or the piper, these also declare His glory—and, as these may be appreciated, so may that as may be given in this world's goods, in power, in might, in moneys, in position—so one may know how, through what channel, one may serve.

Then, keeping the body in such an attunement, aids physically, mentally, and the growth to the soul becomes as one that has made peace with the Creator. These are but little things in the eyes of many. These, by their very foolishness to many, confound the wise. These but make that contentment that makes one seek and seek for knowledge of Him that gives the gifts *in* life; for He be the God of the *living* whom thou servest, and material things are but dead—and are dead *weight* when one has not attuned self to the beauties in every field that makes manifest. *Even* the toad is as beautiful in the sight of the Creator as the lily, and he that heedeth not the little things may not be master of the great things, for he that was capable of using the talents in the little way was made the ruler over *great* cities.

Keep thine body fit. Keep thine mind attuned to beauty.

257-53

When a twenty-four-year-old woman wanted to know how to overcome her fears, Cayce's response suggested that spiritual activities and pursuits would be instrumental in helping her to become more positive:

(Q) How can I become less fearful, and my subconscious mind more able to rest?

(A) As there is brought more and more the activities of the spiritual self through the action of the psychic forces (that is, the creative energy of the subconscious force), this will allow itself to become more and more positive and less and less negative.

911-2

Finally, a fifty-year-old man was given the following advice regarding the power of the mind to heal:

The attitude of the entity, and those dependencies upon creating sufficient numbers of the energized cells—not only in the circulation itself but in the activities of the glandular forces, through the process of the mental relationships of control over the nerve plexus of the body—aided the most; yea, much more than any administration of medicines ... 2976-1

4. Cultivate Systematic Control of Thought

Attitudes become built over time by continuous daily thought processes. With this idea in mind, how might we begin to creatively and constructively restructure such thought processes? The following may prove helpful in this regard:

First, select a negative thought process that you would like to get rid of; for example, self-criticism. Sometimes this takes the form of complaining. Begin on the first day of the week. Promise yourself that during your waking hours you will in no way negate or complain about your situation. Become aware of this commitment day by day. Perhaps you might want to make yourself a little affirmation card or a sticky note pad with a reminder. When you make a mistake or fail, simply go back to your affirmation and try again. Keep checking on yourself.

Now, during this same week, every day make an effort to put into thought, word, and action a thought pattern that you would like to acquire; for example, deliberately try to see something good about each person you meet. And don't stop there—verbalize your positive thoughts to the person and/or to someone else. At least once during the week you might decide to send someone a positive note commenting on the good aspect or quality you have observed in her or him. A little creative thought and practice in this mental exercise can bring a new perspective into your life.

Secondly, you might wish to refer to the following checklist of negative and positive attitudes. This may give you insight into where your thought processes are focused at the present time. If you want to use the checklist as a possible evaluation exercise (and perhaps even ask a partner or a friend to evaluate you as well), you might be able to become more objectively aware of your own strengths and weaknesses. Thereby, deciding to transform the negative thought patterns and reinforce the positive ones.

The positive and negative expressions of energy have been listed under specific centers as a means of suggesting the types of memories and patterns that can be stored at each level. To be sure, the energy or force involved in each expression is the same energy. The difference is how each individual chooses to manifest this energy in different patterns of thought, word, and action. It is *one* energy transformed by individual choice.

The third suggestion is to use a thought reverie that can be helpful in observing and strengthening your own constructive attitudes. The Cayce readings might suggest measuring these attitudes against the highest spiritual ideal, which was defined as the Christ Consciousness—you might also decide to refer to it as spiritual consciousness or even a consciousness of oneness:

(Q) Should the Christ Consciousness be described as the awareness within each soul, imprinted in pattern on the mind and waiting to be awakened by the will, of the soul's oneness with God?
(A) Correct. That's the idea exactly!   5749-14

Take a few minutes (three to five) to review past experiences in your life that best expresses your alignment with qualities of the highest pattern you can awaken within your own mind. The qualities of that pattern are:

- Serves others
- Sees God in every expression of life
- Is obedient to a higher law

Personal Evaluation Chart

Note: to use this chart as the basis for an exercise, rank yourself from 1 to 6 on each positive/negative potential use of energy associated with each of the centers. You might ask a friend to objectively do the same. When you've finished, you can divide the sum for each positive expression row and each negative expression row by 4 in order to calculate the average.

Scoring Key:

1 = Never

2 = Seldom

3 = Occasionally

4 = Frequently

5 = Almost Always

6 = Always

Positive Potential Uses of the Energies Associated with the Centers:

Center	Potential Qualities and Strengths			
Gonads	• Helpful	• Protective	• Serves Others	• Meditates
Cells of Leydig	• Resolute	• Gentle	• Balanced Male/Female Energies	• Merciful
Adrenals	• Seeks Peace with Others	• Persistent	• Faithful	• Controls Temper
Thymus	• Loving Others Before Self	• Generous	• Sympathetic	• Friendly
Thyroid	• Cooperative	• Makes Wise Choices	• Stands by Ideals	• Open to Suggestions
Pineal	• Possesses a Seeking Attitude	• Knows Self	• Reasonable	• Aware of the Oneness of the Divine
Pituitary	• Gives God Credit	• Inspirational	• Humble	• Encourages Others

Negative Potential Uses of the Energies Associated with the Centers:

Center	Potential Faults and Weaknesses			
Gonads	• Self-Indulgent	• Lazy	• Abusive	• Neglects Spiritual Things
Cells of Leydig	• Doubting	• Irresponsible	• Imbalance of Male/Female Energies	• Inflexible
Adrenals	• Overly Protective of Self	• Discouraged	• Domineering	• Angry
Thymus	• Loving Self	• Selfish	• Self-pity	• Withdrawn
Thyroid	• Willful	• Makes Irresponsible Decisions	• Does Not Apply Spiritual Ideals	• Indecisive
Pineal	• Narrow-minded	• Does Not Know Self	• Unreasonable	• Unaware or Indifferent to Oneness
Pituitary	• Self-righteous	• Indifferent	• Arrogant	• Deflates Others

- Is Joyous
- Is Compassionate
- Lives in the present
- Is forgiving
- Is patient
- Is humble

These suggestions are presented with the view of stimulating your own creative ideas for designing techniques that fit your situation and your special needs in beginning to change your attitudes. Give this some thought and begin to work with yourself. Part of you, when stimulated, will cooperate and can draw on help for healing far beyond your present limited range. Then change will begin.

5. Use Inspirational Reading

The conscious mind is busy—indeed, all dimensions of the mind are busy. The mind needs to be busy with ideas that awaken the best in you. Give the mind something to focus upon that offers true inspiration. Many people find the New Testament promises contained in Chapters 14, 15, 16, and 17 of John encouraging. In my own life, I have found that these chapters can be read profitably again and again—they deal directly with fear. Interestingly enough, Edgar Cayce recommended these Bible passages more frequently than any others. He also frequently recommended Psalms 1, 23, 24, 91; Exodus 19; and Deuteronomy 30.

The scriptures of every religion also offer selections for possible study. Return again and again to old favorites when you need to, or find new ones. Some people might decide to read passages from various scriptures, others might focus on uplifting "thoughts for the day," still others might focus on positive affirmations that can be helpful in focusing on building constructive thought processes. If the concept of reincarnation is part of your worldview, some religious selections may have a special appeal to you. Personal favorites of mine include the Bhagavad–Gita of the Hindus and the poems of the Sufi mystics. When asked what Bible passages specifically teach reincarnation, Edgar Cayce replied: "John. Six to eight. Third to fifth. Then the rest as a whole." (452–6) Regardless of the text, search for whatever uplifting material appeals to you to set the stage of your mind for new creative attitudes.

6. Watch Your Dreams as a Means of Observing Your Real Attitude

The Cayce readings stress the importance of working with your dreams, especially as they relate to your body, mind, and spiritual health. Dreams contain all kinds of unobserved psychic phenomena, including clairvoyance, telepathy, precognition, retrocognition (seeing into the past), and even communication with loved ones that have passed away. Dreams can help solve physical, psychological, financial, and spiritual problems. We can gain guidance, advice, and encouragement from our dreams. In fact, the very act of dreaming can be healing, renewing, and revitalizing.

One of the most interesting observations to be found within the approximately 900 references to dreams in the Cayce files is the statement that dreams often reveal our inner attitudes. On one occasion, he explained it in this way:

> **Hence the lessons, as has oft been given, as to how one in one's mental being may create those conditions that bring about just such physical results. But, even as the visions [dreams] are seen, these continue to be mingled together with both good and bad. Just as such thoughts create and bring about such conditions. Then, desist! Either be on the one side or the other, and act that as would bring to self that desired.**   **136-82**

In order to begin working with your dreams, you may find it helpful to start suggesting to yourself, several times before falling asleep, "I will remember my dreams when I awake." Keep a pen and a spiral notebook at your beside and record whatever you can remember upon awakening—even if it's only a feeling. As you go back over and review your dreams every week or so, you will be able to see your attitudes—how they change and how they are reflected in your dreams. For further reference and study, you may wish to explore some of the many excellent books available on dreams.

7. Use Presleep Suggestion

A very practical and helpful technique for dealing with fear from various sources, especially those arising from the unconscious, is giving your self (or others) presleep suggestions just before going to sleep. We have already discussed the use of these suggestions for overcoming fears of various natures. Some of the excerpts that recommend the use of presleep suggestion in overcoming fear include the following:

> (Q) Why do I fear water so that I do not swim far in water over my depth?
> (A) This is from a condition that existed in the subconscious in very young childhood. Suggestions to self, or forcing of self to overcome such, might discharge this from the subconscious influence.
> (Q) Is this why I am afraid to dive or jump into the water even if I am only one foot above the water?
> (A) The same. / 2772-4

> (Q) Is there any way this fear in the body can be removed?
> (A) By the patience, persistence of suggestion to the body. Is there any way that to the mind of a child that has been burned, it can be taught there is a way to handle fire? This is *gradually* builded by the overcoming of fear, through the suggestions— patiently, persistently; patiently, persistently; p*rayerfully*.
> 271-7

> (Q) Why does my daughter [5043] have such a fear of water, and what can I do to eliminate this fear?
> (A) It may only be eliminated by the suggestions that may be made as the daughter turns to sleep. *Make* the suggestions as for the usefulness of water in the experience, else we may have indeed a barren body. 2428-1

For years, individuals exploring the Edgar Cayce material have successfully used the readings' suggestions for presleep suggestion as a means of changing behavioral patterns and overcoming fear. For ex-

ample, one case concerned the behavior of a twelve–year–old–boy. Behaviors that the parents had noticed and hoped to changed included:
inner turmoil, difficulty controlling bowels, fighting with siblings, ver-
bal abuse of his mother, and general hyperactivity. After using the
presleep suggestion approach for twenty–eight days, the boy's mother
wrote:

> In one week there had been such a vast improvement. I couldn't
> believe it was the same boy. Now, with the completion of the first
> 28-day cycle, where he was constantly quarreling and fighting
> with his brothers, he was avoiding situations. Where his terrible
> all-consuming temper had been, he seemed reflective. His great-
> est improvement was in his attitude to me. Previously, he'd come
> from school, change his clothes and go out to play. Then, when
> I'd start supper the terrible fights with his brothers would begin.
> Many an evening ended by my being too ill to eat because of his
> abuse to me. But now (and thank God) he comes from school,
> changes his clothes and *talks to me!* We will sit and discuss a
> problem or he will follow me around as he tells me his thoughts
> or asks what I think. I am once again a part of this child I love!

Suggestions used for self or others as sleep approaches should be
couched in positive, constructive, helpful terms. "No" and "don't" statements only create opposition at the unconscious levels. Positive statements are needed instead. When using the presleep approach, use a low
conversational tone, starting just before the person is asleep and continuing after she or he falls asleep. If giving the suggestions to yourself,
keep repeating the suggestions until you fall asleep. This technique has
repeatedly worked for both children and adults.

8. Develop Your Sense of Humor

A thirty–five–year–old marine once asked Edgar Cayce for help with
his fears; Cayce's reply was that the individual needed to work with
humor:

> (Q) What is the cause of my fear and how may I overcome it?

(A) By seeing the ridiculous and yet the funny side of every experience. Knowing and believing in whom ye have trusted, in the Lord; for without that consciousness of the indwelling, little may ever be accomplished.

(Q) What is the cause of my fear?

(A) Self-condemnation.   5302-1

Here guilt is given as the cause of fear. Our attitude toward ourselves, our willingness to forgive ourselves, is essential to healing fear. One of the most concrete ways of expressing forgiveness is to smile, chuckle, or laugh at oneself. This does not mean a condoning smirk, a wry agreement with the breaking of a law, but rather the recognition of ridiculousness of one's actions, the funny side of the situation.

Edgar Cayce repeatedly spoke of humor as a virtue, something to be cultivated and worked with daily. He admonished one person:

Not as one to be long-faced. For, the earth is the Lord's and the fullness thereof—in *joy!* Do not see the dark side too oft. Turn it over—there's another side to every question. Cultivate in self humor, wit. Ye enjoy it in others, others enjoy it in thee. But too oft it becomes to thee foolishness. *Know* that thy Lord, thy God, *laughed*—even at the Cross.   2995-1

Others were encouraged to cultivate their sense of humor even in the midst of trying experiences:

For, humor—or to be able to see the fun, the ridiculous, in the most sacred experiences to many—is an attribute so well manifested here, but so seldom found in many individuals.   2775-1

Cultivate the ability to see the ridiculous, and to retain the ability to laugh. For, know—only in those that God hath favored is there the ability to laugh, even when clouds of doubt arise, or when every form of disturbance arises.   2984-1

Oftentimes laughter, especially during tension, can provide immediate relief. I am reminded of the many times during the War when a funny, sometimes even vulgar, remark broke great tension and eased the bodies and minds of people gripped in panic and paralyzed by fear. Edgar Cayce noted this virtue in the following comments:

> But Spirit is creative. And while creative influences are about the entity, the greater saving grace of the entity may be said to be its ability to laugh at adversity when others would cry; to be able to make a joke of the most sacred things as well as those that are in the realm of the ridiculous.   1999-1

> In Mercury with Mars we find the high mental abilities, the entity being one who takes all emotions, all conditions and activities very seriously. Yet the entity has within itself the appreciation of humor, seeing the optimistic side as well as the pessimistic side of any experience. Hold to that . . . to that ability to be witty, to show proper wisdom. Quit being too serious. Laugh it off.
> 3685-1

The following comments deal directly with fear:

> One who is at all times inclined towards good humor, and might at times well be called a wit. At *times* the entity sees so *well* the humor in *so many* situations as to appear to see the ridiculous rather than that which is the creative force in humor. *Do not* lose this sense of humor; it will oft be a means for saving *many* an unseeming situation . . .
>   Let that be heeded as first indicated—use rather the turmoils and discouragements *as* a means to keep the wit sharp; and it will be found that creative energies, creative forces, will soon overcome the material turmoils.   2421-2

> First, analyze self. Know that there must be the ability to laugh under the most straining circumstance. There must be the ability to see the sublime as well as the ridiculous.   1823-1

From his state of extended perception, Edgar Cayce saw great value in cultivating a sense of humor:

> The entity should attempt—seriously, prayerfully, spiritually—to see even that as might be called the ridiculous side of every question—the humor in same. Remember that a good laugh, an arousing even to what might in some be called hilariousness, is good for the body, physically, mentally, and gives the opportunity for greater mental and spiritual awakening.
>
> That seriousness with which the body (and mind) takes on the material as well as the mental and social relationships is not good. While the happenings, the experiences even in the material sojourn may have at times tended to convince the body of the seriousness of living, know that life should be joyous, happy, open, and *all* that brings hope . . .
>
> Be *mindful* of the little things, but *do* see the humor, do see the laughable side, and not always the tears, the drab, hard sides. For, there is more than one phase of any problem, any condition, any relationship. Life *is* of the Creative Forces, and an individual uses same for weal or woe.   2647-1

How might you cultivate and develop your own sense of humor? Here are a few suggestions—in all likelihood these may make you think of even more:

Start collecting good jokes and funny stories. Be careful not to use ethnic prejudices and "put-downs" of special groups. Try these stories out on friends and relatives close to you first. Learn how to watch your timing, building suspense and attention. Be careful not to forget the point of the story, which should be related to the conversation or discussion. You may want to begin collecting a file of stories. Read them over now and then. You will discover that you will begin to remember them at the right time.

Excellent sources for humor are the funny papers, sections on jokes in magazines, and books about jokes or humor. The important point is to be aware, be constantly observant, looking for the story or one-liners that can be adapted to situations around you.

Look for the funny things in life—the ridiculous things that happen to you every day. They are happening—you may just not have been observant. As you do this, you will begin to remember past experiences, incidents that as you review them are funny. People will begin to laugh with you, not at you, for their lives are filled with similar incidents that your comments and stories about yourself recall for them. Be careful to be brief, not too long-winded, because the other person may be waiting to tell you a story of her or his own, as well.

Become more observant of animals—pets, wild animals, animals that do things like people—all kinds of animals. They do some funny things. Remember to make notes about funny incidents you have observed. File these with your story collection and review them regularly.

Perhaps most important of all is practice. Never joke with malice, never to put down someone or call attention to weakness, but instead begin to search out the ridiculous side of every conversation and add your contribution of fun to the occasion. You will relieve a great deal of tension in yourself and others. And you will discover a tool for dealing with your fears that works consistently and beautifully.

Overall, the readings emphasize the important role that the mind can play in overcoming personal fears. There are a variety of approaches for cultivating your ability to use the mind as a powerful tool for constructive change. Those approaches include: the use of spiritual ideals, focusing on constructive thoughts, using the mind to influence the body, controlling your thought processes, giving the mind uplifting or inspirational reading, working with dreams, utilizing presleep suggestion, and cultivating a sense of humor. All of these approaches can be effective in overcoming patterns of fear and anxiety while giving the mind much more constructive avenues of expression.

9

Bringing Your Life into Alignment— Physically

The greater disturbance is fear in the body. Then, that to be overcome is the fear of fear.   2952-1

WHETHER OR not a fear is resulting in part from a malfunction or problem within some part of your physical structures or systems, the regular tune-up and alignment of your body can only be helpful. In order to obtain a balance in the physical body, the readings often recommended such things as diet, exercise, massage, various physical therapies, maintaining a balanced lifestyle and, of course, making an appointment with a physician, osteopath, or chiropractor. Some of the suggestions Cayce frequently detailed, included the following:

Maintain a Balanced and Nutritious Diet

Nearly every individual who came to Edgar Cayce for help from a physical reading was given dietary suggestions. Overall, those suggestions included:
- Plenty of fruits and vegetables
- A limited amount of red meats and starches
- A diet that was more alkaline-producing (as opposed to acid-producing)
- Refraining from great quantities of sweets and pastries
- Getting at least six to eight glasses of water each day
- Keeping in mind the importance of not combining certain foods at the same meal
- Moderation in all things

Specific advice for menu planning generally included recommendations such as the following:

Breakfast: Citrus fruits or juices and brown, whole-wheat toast. Alternately, individuals were told that they could have cooked cereals and milk, or whole-wheat or cracked wheat cereals, but never to eat cereals and citrus fruits and juices at the same meal. Coffee or tea could also be taken at breakfast but Cayce suggested that it was important never to use cream or milk in either beverage.

Lunch: The combination of a variety of fresh, raw vegetables. The readings suggested that one meal each day should consist wholly of green or raw vegetables, such as lettuce, celery, carrots, beets, peas, lentils, tomatoes, spinach, and vegetables that could be made into a salad. Salad dressings made with oil were preferable to cream or milk based dressings. Graham or whole-wheat wafers or crackers could also be eaten at the same time. If desired, individuals were often told that they could have a small amount of coffee or tea at the end of the meal.

Dinner: Cooked vegetables, especially the inclusion of leafy vegetables was recommended in the evening. It was suggested that vegetables were to be cooked in their own juices, in a steamer, or in Patapar paper. If meat is a part of your diet, the readings generally recommended that chicken, fowl, seafood, or lamb (as opposed to beef) were to be taken at the evening meal. In preparing meats, the readings suggested that they were to be broiled, boiled, baked, stewed, or scalloped rather than fried.

In addition to the above dietary suggestions, Edgar Cayce often stated that a familiar rhyme would be very good advice for most individuals to follow. That rhyme goes as follows: "After breakfast work a while, after lunch rest a while, after dinner walk a mile." (470-17, 1158-11, 3624-1, and others)

Commit to and Maintain a Personal Exercise Program

Although the need for individuals to exercise has become a common pronouncement, Edgar Cayce was years ahead of his time when he suggested how important it was for individuals to incorporate exercise into their daily lifestyles. Frequent suggestions for exercise included gentle limbering, stretching, and breathing exercises. Oftentimes, the readings suggested stretching exercises like those done by a cat upon awakening. Common exercises that were recommended included brisk walking, swimming, handball, tennis, golf, and horseback riding.

A primary purpose of exercise is to help the body's circulation. With circulation in mind, the readings often encouraged individuals to work with exercises that would stretch their upper body, torso, arms, and abdomen in the morning and their lower body and legs in the evening just before retiring. Exercise advice given to specific individuals along these lines included the following:

> As we find, we would take the exercise that has been once indicated; something of the setting-up exercises. Of mornings exercise those portions of the body particularly above the hips, or from the torso portion up, see? The raising of the arms, the bending to the side, to the front, the circular motions of the head, neck, the circular motions of the arms. Then of an evening just before retiring exercise the lower portion of the body. These will

tend to make for the more perfect coordination in all the muscular forces of the system, will tend to make for the ability of the superficial circulation as coordinating with the deeper to adjust all of these conditions.   416-9

In the morning take exercise of the upper portion of the body, from the waist up—circulation from the waist up, raising and lowering the arms—raising them high above head, as to scratch—then take the head and neck exercise, and if one is left off leave off the body, but do not leave off the head and neck exercise! but take them all! In the evening take the stooping exercise and bending for the lower portion of the body, or the swinging of the lower limbs.   257-167

Raise the arms, rocking back and forth on the heel and toe. Gradually, as the body raises up, raise the arms high also. Such an exercise is most beneficial.   1620-3

Make Certain That Your Spine Is in Alignment

The Edgar Cayce readings place a great deal of emphasis on the need for individuals to keep their spine in alignment. Therefore, a careful spinal checkup with a good osteopath or chiropractor followed up by periodic sessions may be important to you. Try various therapists until you find one that satisfies you, as oftentimes each professional works in different ways. You need to be in rapport with people who touch your body. Some are better channels of healing than others.

The readings often recommended examinations and treatment at the third cervical, the ninth dorsal, and the sacral–coccyx areas. Oftentimes they were concerned with the cerebrospinal–sympathetic nerve plexus and circulation to the endocrine glands. You may find it helpful to take time to look at your doctor's charts or to read and discover more information about your glands.

If you have never had an adjustment before, you may decide to take a series of three or four adjustments, just to see the results. Then, about every three or four months, have another check-up, whether or not you think you need it. This is especially true for any individual who thinks that his or her body may be contributing to the source of fear patterns.

Treat Yourself to Massage and Light Sweats

The Cayce information on health and healing is a strong proponent of individuals receiving massage and light sweats. Both can be extremely important for facilitating the release and elimination of body toxins and for increasing circulation. In addition to making an individual feel better and more relaxed, Cayce suggested that massage could provide individuals with increased energy as well as ward off health problems, such as arthritis.

As many practitioners have their own style, you may find it helpful to be massaged by different therapists until you find one that is best suited for you. You may also wish to learn some techniques and share them with family members and friends, exchanging massages in the process. You might be surprised by how many individuals are interested in this idea. A.R.E., the Cayce headquarters in Virginia Beach, also offers a variety of massage services and programs, including the Cayce/Reilly School of Massotherapy where individuals are trained to become massage therapists. More information is available from A.R.E. or from the web site: www.edgarcayce.org.

Light sweats can often be secured at health spas or by some massage therapists. A hot tub bath or Epsom salts bath can also be helpful before a massage or by itself. These sweats are especially helpful at enabling the body to release toxins and poisons.

Maintain a Balanced Lifestyle

The Cayce information on health has often been summarized by the acronym C.A.R.E., suggesting the importance of Circulation, Assimilation, Relaxation, and Elimination in maintaining a balanced and healthy body. In addition to a healthy physical balance, the readings are adamant in encouraging individuals to be balanced in all aspects of their lives—balancing work, home, family, relaxation, rest, and so forth.

The following advice was given to a forty-five-year-old banker who had neglected finding balance in his own life. It beautifully sums up the importance of balance:

> We find that these arose as a result of what might be called occupational disturbances; not enough in the sun, not enough of hard work. Plenty of brain work, but the body is supposed to coordinate the spiritual, mental and physical. He who does not give recreation a place in his life, and the proper tone to each phase—well, he just fools self and will some day—as in this body in the present—be paying the price. There must be a certain amount of recreation. There must be certain amounts of rest. These are physical, mental and spiritual necessities.   3352-1

Have a Physician Give You a Checkup on Your Endocrines

This suggestion is primarily for those who are faced with fears related to tensions, nervousness, frequent or unusual tiredness, distorted perception of voices or visual hallucinations, or unwanted and uncontrollable psychic experiences. Considering that some of the most difficult and disturbing of the fear patterns discussed by Edgar Cayce concern glandular disturbances, this may be an important step in finding treatment. The thyroid gland and the adrenals should be especially considered. In some instances, your chiropractor or osteopath can handle these tests for you. Or you may also want to discuss the matter with your family physician.

As you consider and contemplate the cause and treatment of fear and anxiety, you will begin to understand the importance of dealing with the whole person. The physical body, the mind (conscious and unconscious), the emotions, and the spirit are all interwoven. We need to begin thinking of ourselves as one whole—body, mind, and soul. From Edgar Cayce's perspective, an understanding of this oneness is essential.

10

The Oneness of All Force

The first lesson for six months should be ONE—One—One—ONE;
Oneness of God, oneness of man's relation, oneness of force,
oneness of time, oneness of purpose, ONENESS in every effort—
Oneness—Oneness!   900-429

HAVE YOU ever had the experience of looking into another
person's eyes and suddenly found yourself somehow merging
with that individual? Perhaps, for a moment, the "outer you"
ceased to be the focus of your consciousness. You became absorbed
into something greater than yourself; time and space became one; you
were focused in an eternal now.

For many individuals this type of experience has also happened in
nature. Sensing this union with something greater than one's self can
occur by staring at a starry sky on a clear, cold night. It might be experienced by watching a shaft of sunlight dance atop a bubbling brook.

Some have felt this union by watching a moon over a restless ocean or by listening to the high notes of a mockingbird. Frequently, individuals can relate to the experience by staring deeply into the eyes of a pet that stares back at them with total and unconditional love. Those who love the outdoors can sometimes hear it in the rustling of corn stalks on a hot, summer afternoon, or by becoming aware of the strange sounds of a massive tree that seems to come alive with the rustling of a breeze. Much of the mystical literature of the world is filled with such descriptions of union and oneness.

I believe that many of these experiences are simply glimpses of a fundamental reality—the oneness of all Creation. This principle is relevant to the subjects of fear and anxiety because many fears originate due to our failure to comprehend this universal law.

Ultimately, all force or energy is from one universal source, which the readings define as *Spirit*. Two reasons that this oneness seems so fractured to the material mind is because of: (1) our rebellion against God's creative will, both in and outside of this material plane, and (2) the limitations of our consciousness in the material world. In terms of how this oneness impacts our relationship and connection to God, the answer was given in response to a forty-seven-year-old woman's question about the nature of God:

(Q) Is it correct when praying to think of God as impersonal force or energy, everywhere present; or as an intelligent listening mind, which is aware of every individual on earth and who intimately knows everyone's needs and how to meet them?

(A) Both! For He is also the energies in the finite moving in material manifestation. He is also the Infinite, with the awareness. And thus as ye attune thy own consciousness, thy own awareness, the unfoldment of the presence within beareth witness with the presence without. And as the Son gave, "I and my Father are one," then ye come to know that ye and thy Father are one, as ye abide in Him.

Thus we find the manifestations of life, the manifestations of energy, the manifestations of power that *moves* in material, are the representation, the manifestation of the Infinite God . . .

> **For until ye become as a savior, as a help to some soul that has lost hope, lost its way, ye do not fully comprehend the God within, the God without.**   **1158-14**

Throughout many of the more than 14,000 Edgar Cayce readings there are clearly defined expressions of this principle of the Oneness of all force. For example, a thirty–one–year–old stockbroker was told that this principle was not only important for every spiritual journey but that it was just as applicable from material, mental, and moral perspectives. In every endeavor and experience this law of oneness must be taken into consideration. The reading went on to say that even when an individual understood the principle, the greatest challenge became one of simply applying it in everyday life (900–280).

Consider also the following from an Edgar Cayce reading given to a forty–seven–year–old man in 1943:

> **Each soul has within its power that to use which may make it at one with Creative Forces or God . . .**
>
> **For, man in his nature—physical, mental and spiritual—is a replica, is a part of whole universal reaction in materiality.**
>
> **Hence there are those elements which if applied in a material way, if there is the activity with same of the spirit and mind, may bring into the experience of each atom of the body force or cell itself the awareness of the Creative Force or God.**   **3492-1**

That same year, Cayce told a forty–five–year–old woman:

> **For ye are made body, mind, soul. They each have their part in thy oneness, or they are one; as Father, Son, and Holy Spirit is one.**   **3051-3**

Interestingly enough, in a reading given to another woman, Cayce suggested it was because she had ignored this law of oneness that various aspects of her life were in conflict and fear had come as a result:

> **(Q) What has caused the recurrent experiences of waking during**

the night screaming? Explain these experiences and advise the
body as to just what to do about them.
(A) Looking into self and the choices, which have been made
respecting the spiritual import, you will find that there has been
a conflict between the activity of the flesh and the mental and
spiritual self. These produce upon the emotional self, fear. These
may only be wholly eliminated by making the mental and
spiritual mind and the material or physical body coordinant,
cooperative, consistent one with another.   1315-10

From Cayce's perspective, we are souls, spiritual beings having an
earthly experience. Essentially, our purpose for being in the earth is to
gather experiences and lessons in soul growth that will enable us to
return to an awareness of our spiritual selves—or God consciousness.
Ultimately, Cayce described each of us at the soul level as being com-
posed of a spirit, a mind, and a will. *Spirit* is seen as our individual
expression or connection to the One Force. The *Mind* is the building
block that enables patterns of thought to take shape and eventually
manifest in our physical lives. The *Will* is that element of choice that
selects and determines the individual choices and directions we make
each moment of every day. To some degree, our present state of awareness or confusion as we try to understand the oneness of all force seems
to lie in how we have used our free will:

These are in the experience of each soul. And what the entity does
about that free will that is the heritage of each soul, as its *birthright*—
the *will*—makes for development or retardment; and nothing may
separate thee from the knowledge of the Father but thyself! 1219-1

For the will is that with which each soul makes or loses the
opportunities which are its birthright in each experience. For He
hath not willed that any soul should perish, and it is not by chance
that the soul is in the environ but that in the use of its concept
of that creative force of which it is a part it is brought along that
line, that sphere, that awareness, that consciousness in which it
finds itself.   1770-2

For—body, mind, soul—body, mind, spirit—physical, mental, spiritual—these are phases of individual experience. They each have
their duties, their obligations, their limitations, their abilities,
their desires, their hopes. But *will*—Will—with the spiritual
influence which is the birthright of every soul, combined with
material activity—may bring into the experience of self, of others,
the fulfilling of those obligations, of duties, of love, of hope—yea,
of fear—and eternal life.   1885-2

Within all of us, quite different forces or energies sometimes seem to
be in conflict. Anger floods our minds, sweeping away reason, and we
may find that we want to strike another person with thought, word, or
act. But what if this was the very same energy that could be used to care
for a sick friend? Is the passion of sexual drive the same energy we use
to create a beautiful picture or poem? Can the destructive energy of
self-pity be the same energy that is used for healing prayer? The Edgar
Cayce material says yes. There is only one energy. We direct this one
energy through various centers of the body; it only seems different
because of its level of expression.

When we look beyond ourselves to other people, it is difficult for us
not to see divisions of forces. Racial differences, the color of skins, cus-
toms, and religious beliefs are only a few of these divisions. It is sometimes hard to look beyond our fears and prejudices to see people as
being much like us. However, the Cayce information challenges us to
find God through the concepts of our selves and our relationships with
others.

Let the law of the *Lord*, as *thou knowest* it in thine heart, *be* the
rule of *thy* life—and thy dealings with thy fellow man! And ye will
find that the growth of the mind-spiritual, of the mind-mental, of
the body-physical, will open the way for thee, day by day.

For, as those laws that become as but watchwords to many on
the tower, there is a whole day's work before thee each day, with
all its glorious opportunities of seeing the glory of the Lord
manifested by thine own acts!

Yet if that which confronts thee makes for discouragement,

harshness of words, lack of enthusiasm, or those things that make for doubts or fears, the opportunity has turned its back—and what *is* the outlook? Doubt and fear!

Study, then, to show thyself approved, *each day! Do what* thou *knowest* to do, to be aright! Then *leave it alone!* God giveth the increase! Thy worry, thy anxiety, only will produce disorder in thine *own* mind!

For the application in self, the *try*, the effort, the energy expended in the proper direction, is all that is required of *thee*.

601-11

. . . for through self man will understand its Maker when it understands its relation to its Maker, and it will only understand that through itself, and that understanding is the knowledge as is given here in this state.

Each and every person getting that understanding has its individual force toward the great creation, and its individual niche, place or unit to perform . . . yet the understanding for the individual entity, viewed from its own standpoint, with its knowledge, is obtained and made ready by itself, to be manifested through itself, towards its own development, and in that development of the creation or world.   3744-5

"What?" we might ask ourselves is the meaning of our "niche, place, or unit to perform?" For me, these words suggest that each individual life experience has important and special meaning. However simple or complex any incarnation on earth can be, we are responsible for applying whatever we perceive of God's laws. It is not enough to know—we must daily apply love, patience, kindness, and so forth. As I understand the Cayce information, it is not God Who has created chaos on earth; instead, we have too often failed to fulfill the role for which we were created. At a subconscious level, we sense this failure to measure up, we sense our inadequacy, and we become afraid.

However, it is possible for us to realize the fundamental principle of oneness in our lives and in our interactions with others; in fact, it is highly desirable that we do so, by developing and expressing the creative force within ourselves. This can be done, in part, through self-examination and personal growth. As we achieve higher levels of consciousness, we can begin to become aware of a new relationship to all nature and to all people everywhere. Step by step, we can begin to transform the energy from the negative modes of expression, self-pity, anger, hate, fear, into creative thought, word, and action and even into love, patience, and joy. By so doing, we will truly know the Oneness that has been spoken to us from times of old: "Hear, O Israel: The Lord our God is one Lord." (Deuteronomy 6:4)

Conclusion

As has been give, "Fear not." Keep the faith; for those that be with thee are greater than those that would hinder.   294-185

FEAR AND anxiety have many different manifestations. Fear patterns become so entangled in our lives that tracing them or identifying the nature of our anxieties may become difficult. Do not become trapped by fixating your attention on the need to find possible causes. Instead, begin to transform the negative, sometimes even strangely fascinating, feelings of fear to change your life. You can transform anxiety and fear energies to constructive thoughts and actions. My experience suggests that persistent work with the concepts explored in this book can bring not only freedom from fear, but also releases new energies that enable us to lead richer, fuller lives.

From the perspective of the Edgar Cayce readings, fear is perhaps the most detrimental force in preventing individuals from fulfilling the purpose for which they were created. Therefore, overcoming fear and anxiety is not only desirous but it instead becomes essential. To this end, Cayce repeatedly assured individuals that transforming fear patterns into more creative forms of expression was absolutely possible.

> **Fear the greatest bugaboo to the human elements, for in fear comes those conditions that destroy . . . To *overcome* fear, so fill the mental forces with that of the creative nature as to cast out fear; for he, or she, that is without fear is free indeed, and perfect love casteth out fear.**   **5439-1**

The unconscious mind is oftentimes a battlefield. Conflicts between aspects of ourselves create our fears. Our desires war with our tendencies to repress them; our real worlds struggle with our imaginary worlds; we are torn between our drive to be important and our sense of insignificance; we hope for acceptance but confront rejection; sometimes we want to live, sometimes we want to die.

Fear symptoms arise from bodily stress, psychological childhood conditioning, and the stress of daily living. Fears may even arise to haunt us from previous lives. We also fear annihilation and death. Finally, each of us at some point in our lives feels a sense of failure that grows out of the sameness of existence and a threat of meaninglessness.

The Edgar Cayce readings speak to many of these fears and provide, for many people, ways to deal with them. For example, an important spiritual law can help renew our relationship with our Creator—the oneness of all force. We can begin to sense that we are part of a whole and that we do have a part to play as children of God—even as co-creators with Him. Moreover, through prayer and meditation, we can begin to awaken the real soul self. It's possible to arouse our wills and to take control of the mind. As we set ideals, we can measure our thoughts, our words, and our actions against those ideals. We can build fear-free constructive attitudes by ceasing to feel negative thought patterns; tuning up our flesh bodies; conscientiously trying to be positive and constructive in our thinking; checking our dreams to observe what we are building with the mind; using positive suggestions on self; spending time with inspirational reading; and developing a sense of humor. We can use small groups for protection, help with self–observation, and healing. And service to others—however we wish to define that—needs to be incorporated into our daily lives.

This book has been written for you. If you were a person who was desperately sick, you would not have come this far. You are not alone. Fear is a universal pattern arising from our rebelliousness. Our thought forms and our focus on the physical aspect of life can both block our perception of the real goal of existence. Yet, as we move in consciousness, we can come to know our Creator and a true relationship of love with our fellow human beings. We have shut ourselves off from God; we are guilt–ridden, unable to accept God's constant love for us, so we sometimes find it difficult to love our selves or others.

What is most exciting about the Edgar Cayce information given to individuals with fear and anxiety is that these problems can be overcome. Not only did the readings provide practical advice for helping individuals conquer and heal every imaginable fear but I have seen how advice given years ago to specific individuals continues to help people from all backgrounds even today. The Cayce concepts suggest that our destructive fear energy can be transformed into constructive drives, freeing us to become more loving, more creative, and more in touch with the spiritual nature that is part of us all.

No one idea, prescription, or action will completely resolve any anxiety or fear. These emotions are entangled in our bodies, our minds, our emotions, and even our spiritual lives. To overcome them, we need to change all of our patterns of life activity. This awareness will enable us to understand new dimensions regarding the self. Turning loose, letting go of our negative past, and beginning *now* to rebuild new patterns of physical, mental, and spiritual activities can free us from anxieties and fears that hold us chained in a consciousness of inadequacy and even self–destruction. The time has come to take seriously the Gospel's admonition: "Let not your heart be troubled, neither let it be afraid." (John 14:27)

I wish you every encouragement, good wish, and blessing as you continue this journey we call life.

Appendix A:
Fear Questionnaire

Getting in Touch with Possible Causes for Personal Fears

Y	N	Answer each question or statement with either "Yes" or "No."
		1. Have you ever had a severe accident?
		2. Do you feel uncomfortable in the presence of clergy, ministers, rabbis, nuns, or priests?
		3. Do you remember an especially bad childhood experience involving fear?
		4. I am unable to define my goals in life.
		5. Have you ever been frightened by what you thought was a ghost?
		6. Do you frequently wake up feeling tired and unprepared for the day's activities?

Y	N	
		7. Have you ever been afraid of any particular race of people?
		8. Were you ever punished severely in childhood?
		9. I do not believe I have freedom of choice in life.
		10. While going to sleep or being placed under anesthesia have you ever been disturbed by the fear of whether or not you were going to wake up?
		11. Would you consider yourself as being highly excitable?
		12. Would you be hesitant or afraid to wear a costume from some period in history for a "come as you were" party?
		13. Do you have fear dreams or nightmares in the present that involve you as a child?
		14. Have you abandoned or broken with your early childhood religious or spiritual upbringing?
		15. Would you be upset with the idea of having to touch a corpse?
		16. Do you talk rapidly or excessively?
		17. Have you ever been repulsed or afraid of any particular group of people, such as soldiers, beggars, crippled individuals, policemen, etc.?
		18. I recall a childhood incident when an adult or an older child horribly frightened me.
		19. Do you feel guilty for not living up to what God expects of you?
		20. Have you ever been worried about going to hell?
		21. Do you have periods of utter exhaustion?
		22. When you enter a museum, is there a particular culture that you especially want to avoid?

Y	N	
		23. Is there any period in your childhood about which you have no memory?
		24. Do you frequently think that God has given up on humankind?
		25. Do you believe that death is the end of everything?
		26. Have your sexual drives ever tended toward feelings or indications of violence?
		27. Are you afraid of any particular animal or insect?
		28. When you were a child, do you remember ever being severely frightened by a dog, horse, or other animal?
		29. I'm not certain whether or not God requires certain things of us.
		30. Have you ever worried about what happened to someone close to you who died?
		31. I dislike my physical body.
		32. Do you have a fear of primitive cultures?
		33. As a child, did you ever wake up screaming?
		34. Would you rather not have an experience in nature in which you felt that you were brought closer to the Creator?
		35. Do you worry about losing someone close to you through death?
		36. Are you aware of any irregularity of the functioning of your thyroid gland?
		37. Do you have an abhorrence or fear of any weapons such as guns, knives, clubs, etc.?
		38. As a child did you ever think that you were adopted or worry because you really were adopted?
		39. Do you believe that prayers only have a psychological effect?

Y	N	
		40. Have you ever felt responsible for the death of another person?
		41. I have headaches fairly regularly.
		42. Have you ever deliberately avoided books, plays, or movies about any particular country or class of people?
		43. Were you ever lost as a child?
		44. Have you ever been afraid of God?
		45. Do you have a fear of graveyards, funeral parlors, undertakers, etc.?
		46. Have you ever had a pain or a soreness in your spine that lasted more than a few days or weeks?
		47. As a child, were you ever afraid of someone that you knew?
		48. When I was young, I was often shy around adults or other children.
		49. I think that people who believe God is a personal being or an impersonal energy are only fooling themselves.
		50. Would it frighten you to communicate with a dead person?
		51. Are you afraid of losing control of your emotions?
		52. Do you have a fear of confinement in places like hospitals, jails, mental institutions?
		53. Did you have an unhappy childhood?
		54. Are you worried that you have not been "saved," in the sense of being "born again" with a personal relationship with Jesus/God?
		55. Do you have a uneasy or horrible memory of having had to watch a person die?

Y	N	
		56. Are you afraid of "giving in" to a forbidden impulse?
		57. Do you fear or shy away from very poor people or very wealthy people?
		58. When you were between the ages of 6 and 20, do you remember any child that you truly hated?
		59. I don't believe that Jesus was a highly evolved soul, if he existed at all.
		60. I feel that I am unprepared to die.

Scoring: Circle the numbers that you answered with a "Yes," and tabulate the totals that you have (0-12) in each row (the key can be found at the bottom of this page):

	1	6	11	16	21	26	31	36	41	46	51	56
A = _____	1	6	11	16	21	26	31	36	41	46	51	56
B = _____	2	7	12	17	22	27	32	37	42	47	52	57
C = _____	3	8	13	18	23	28	33	38	43	48	53	58
D = _____	4	9	14	19	24	29	34	39	44	49	54	59
E = _____	5	10	15	20	25	30	35	40	45	50	55	60

Key—Possible Sources of Fears:

A = Possible fears due to a physical situation or problem

B = Possible fears due to a past life experience

C = Possible repressed fears from childhood

D = Possible fears of religion or God

E = Possible fears of death or the unknown

Appendix B:
Bringing All Things to
Your Remembrance

I **N ORDER** to discover the root of personal fears and anxieties it's possible to become an observer in your own private laboratory. Although not taking the place of the need for personal counseling, such a process can often assist an individual in coming to terms with many fears and anxieties that can be addressed by the individual self. In my own experience, a three-part self-study process that I have used and have often shared with others has been extremely helpful.

First, set aside a regular daily period for prayer and meditation. For those who are new to the discipline of meditation, I have often recommended the "Meditation" chapter in the *A Search for God*[1] books, created

---

[1] Association for Research and Enlightenment, Inc. *A Search for God*, Books 1 and 2. Virginia Beach, VA. A.R.E. Press. 1992.

by an original group that studied the Cayce information on prayer, meditation, and personal development. Individuals may also wish to take advantage of A.R.E.'s worldwide Study Group program—finding a group of individuals nearby or online that are studying Cayce's concepts of personal growth and development.

Second, begin keeping a personal dream journal by your bedside, cultivating the habit of recording all of your dreams. Put your journal where you can reach it first thing in the morning. Your dreams can provide amazing insights into levels of consciousness, memories, and insights for personal healing and transformation.

Third, after thirty days of working with prayer, meditation, and your personal dreams, take time to write down the answers to this emotional questionnaire. Answer each question from the perspective of your *feelings* rather than simply your thoughts about the question. For many individuals, this process has proven to be a much more exciting adventure than they first realized. Give it a thorough test!

A Questionnaire to Help You Examine Your Emotional Urges:

1. Describe any personal weakness that has persisted or recurred in your experience.

2. How do you feel about this weakness?

3. Is there one of your five senses (sight, hearing, taste, smell, touch) that is keener or more developed than the others? Name it and give an example.

4. Do you truly enjoy any particular reaction at the level of your senses? Describe.

5. Is there any particular food or way of cooking food that you especially enjoy?

6. Are there any physical body types of people to which you are drawn or repelled? Explain.

7. Do movies dealing with any particular type of physical activity appeal to you? Name one or more such movies that you have been drawn to.

8. Is there any type of physical activity that you enjoy reading about?

9. What is your most outstanding body skill or dexterity?

10. Think back to a time when you had a physical fight with another person. Did you enjoy it or did you instead try to pull away from the experience?

11. Have you ever disliked a person? What physical characteristics or traits about that person do you remember?

12. Do you have any body habits that others have complained about?

13. What physical characteristics do you look for and admire in others?

14. List the body habits or disciplines that you make a conscious effort to maintain.

15. What particular weakness or physical lack do you most often complain about?

16. What body habits do you have that, in your opinion, are unlike most of the people you know?

17. Is there any particular physical activity that you find especially exciting and stimulating, that creates, in thought or participation, strong emotional enjoyment?

18. What physical ability do you wish for or have you striven to acquire?

19. Is there any particular physical injury or weakness you are afraid of having to face?

20. What physical (body) weakness or handicap do you notice most in others? Describe how you feel about people with that physical weakness or handicap.

21. Do you especially enjoy the food of any particular country or region? What is your mood most often when you are eating this type of food?

22. Do you enjoy cooking or eating food that has been prepared outdoors, in the open?

23. Have you at any time worn a great deal of jewelry? Worn your hair in some special fashion? Describe. Attributed great sentiment or real value to some physical object? Have you worn or liked long fingernails?

24. Do you have a special interest or dislike of any country? Explain. Does this interest express itself in decorations in your home, interest in travel or books you read, and so on? Describe and explain fully.

25. When you go to a museum, what section do you visit first, and where do you spend most of your time?

26. Do you feel drawn to or repelled by any class, race, or religious group of people? What do you most like or dislike about them?

27. Do you especially like or dislike any phase of church or worship activity? Describe and explain such things as your first experience with the activity, your age, your reaction, and so on.

28. Have you ever had a personal religious experience? Describe, giving age, nature of experience, and so forth.

29. Is there any section of the country that strongly appeals to you?

30. Have you ever read a historical book or novel about a country or a group of people that strongly appealed to you? Describe your feelings about the experience.

31. Do you remember some of the movies that have deeply touched you emotionally? What was the subject of those movies?

32. What is your most absorbing hobby at the present time? How much time do you spend on that hobby? Do you know others that have the same hobby you do?

33. How much time do you spend alone? Do you enjoy being alone?

34. Do you make an effort to be outdoors? Do you make an effort to spend time indoors, perhaps reading or spending time alone?

35. Do you receive much excitement or enjoyment from any type of group games or activities?

36. Is there a problem in your life that has recurred repeatedly?

37. Is there some favorable experience or condition that has recurred repeatedly in your life?

38. What faults and weaknesses do you notice most in others?

39. What qualities and strengths do you notice most in others?

40. Is there any type of person that you are afraid of?

41. What kinds of activities or experiences are you afraid of, make you anxious, or you simply try to avoid?

42. What do you fear the most in life?

43. What do you complain about the most?

44. What types of music do you enjoy the most? How much time do you spend listening to music and can you describe any outstanding experience that occurred to you while listening to music?

45. Describe any dreams you have had about people, places, events, or periods in history that have occurred repeatedly.

46. In your opinion, what is your greatest talent?

47. In your opinion, what is your greatest weakness?

48. Are there people that you have been suddenly and emotionally attracted to or felt that you know immediately?

49. Are there people that you have been suddenly and emotionally afraid of or anxious about being around as soon as you met them?

50. Describe any of the experiences you have had that may be evidence of your own past lives.

Your answers to these questions can provide you with a wealth of information about your self, your likes and dislikes, your strengths and weaknesses, and your qualities and faults. Taken together, the information should provide you with insights and clues about your past lives: what you were doing, where you were, what you learned, and the habits and qualities you acquired. By correlating dream images with some of this information, you may even be able to piece together more details. You can even specifically ask for dream help to provide further insights into a past life or a past relationship.

This exercise might also prompt you to continue searching to know your self. Insights from psychics, from people who know you well, and from your continued spiritual search can also be valuable. Ongoing meditation can help to unlock memories from your subconscious mind. You may also decide to try a hypnotic regression or an imaginative reverie designed to bring past-life images to your present consciousness.

As you truly strive to understand your relationships, develop your talents and abilities, overcome your weaknesses, and conquer your old fears, it is possible to "bring all things to your remembrance" (John 14:26) and come to know your self, your relationship to others, and your connection to God.

Appendix C:
References and Recommended Reading

Anonymous. *The Boy Who Saw True*. Essex, England: The C.W. Daniel Company Limited. 1988.

Association for Research and Enlightenment, Inc. *A Search for God*, Books 1 and 2. Virginia Beach, VA. A.R.E. Press. 1992.

Atwater, P.M.H. *Coming Back to Life: The After-Effects of the Near-Death Experience*. New York: Ballantine Books. 1988.

Bowman, Carol. *Children's Past Lives: How Past Life Memories Affect Your Child*. New York: Bantam Books. 1998.

Cayce, Hugh Lynn. *Venture Inward*. New York: Perennial Library (Harper & Row). 1964.

Cerminara, Gina. *Many Mansions*. New York: NY: New American Library. 1967.

Grant, Robert J. *The Place We Call Home: Exploring the Soul's Existence After Death*. Virginia Beach, VA: A.R.E. Press. 2000.

Greaves, Helen. *Testimony of Light*. Essex, England: The C.W. Daniel Company Limited. 1969.

The Holy Bible, King James Version. 1979.

Kübler-Ross, Elisabeth. *On Death and Dying*. New York: Collier Books, MacMillan Publishing Company. 1969.

McGarey, Gladys, T., M.D. *Born to Live*. Phoenix, Arizona: Gabriel Press. 1980.

Moody, Raymond A. Jr., M.D. *Life After Life*. New York: Bantam Books. 1977.

Stevenson, Ian, M.D. *Twenty Cases Suggestive of Reincarnation*. Charlottesville, VA: University Press of Virginia. 1974.

Sugrue, Thomas. *There is a River*. Virginia Beach, VA: A.R.E. Press. 1997.

Todeschi, Kevin J. *Edgar Cayce on Soul Development*. Virginia Beach, VA: A.R.E. Press. 2004.